Origami
Japanese Paper Folding

By Florence Sakade

TUTTLE PUBLISHING
Tokyo • Rutland, Vermont • Singapore

Published by Tuttle Publishing, an Imprint of
Periplus Editions (HK) Ltd.,with editorial offices
at 364 Innovation Drive, North Clarendon,
VT 05759 and 130 Joo Seng Road, #06–01,
Singapore 368357.

©1958, 2002 Charles E. Tuttle Company Inc.

Library of Congress Catalog No. 2002103227
ISBN-10: 0-8048-3308-7
ISBN-13: 978-0-8048-3308-0

First published in three volumes 1957–9
Second edition 2002

09 08 07 06
9 8 7 6 5 4

Printed in Singapore

TUTTLE PUBLISHING® is a registered trademark of
Tuttle Publishing, a division of Periplus Editions (HK) Ltd.

Distributed by:

North America, Latin America & Europe
Tuttle Publishing
364 Innovation Drive
North Clarendon, VT 05759-9436
Tel: (802) 773 8930; Fax: (802) 773 6993
Email: info@tuttlepublishing.com
www.tuttlepublishing.com

Japan
Tuttle Publishing
Yaekari Building, 3rd Floor
5-4-12 Osaki, Shinagawa-ku
Tokyo 141-0032
Tel: (03) 5437 0171; Fax; (03) 5437 0755
Email: tuttle-sales@gol.com

Asia Pacific
Berkeley Books Pte. Ltd.
130 Joo Seng Road, #06-01,
Singapore 368357.
Tel: (65) 6280 1330; Fax: (65) 6280 6290
Email; inquires@periplus.com.sg
www.periplus.com

Contents

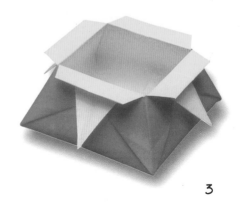

Introduction

ORIGAMI, THE STIMULATING HOBBY of paper folding, has a long tradition in Japan. For more than ten centuries, it has been a favorite pastime with Japanese children and continues to occupy an important place in their lives. Even the youngest Japanese child can create intricate figures through step-by-step foldings of square pieces of colored paper. Some become so skilled that they can fold an object such as a bird from a one-inch square of paper or from the wrappings of candies. Origami objects are regularly used to decorate gifts, to adorn noticeboards in school classrooms, and as part of the displays in shops.

The fascinating art of origami is no longer confined to Japan but has spread throughout the world. It is particularly popular with children and adults in the US. While a child enjoys origami as a pleasurable pastime, parents and teachers can see that paper folding has definite educational value. The ability to follow directions, for example, is an invaluable tool—and advantage—throughout school life as well as afterwards in the workplace and elsewhere. With origami, the child learns that he must follow the directions exactly in order to achieve the desired result. This means he also develops patience. Moreover, origami calls for accuracy and concentrated attention, as the proper shapes can be obtained only through careful, symmetrical foldings. Because the child must also select the most suitable colors for his projects from among those available, he develops an awareness of harmony and a greater appreciation of the world around him. Japanese paper folding thus offers not only hours of peaceful recreation and that indescribable pleasure of accomplishment when a solid figure has been made from a little piece of paper, but it also forms the mind and gives control and skill to the fingers of those who enjoy it.

The objects in this book can be folded even by beginners after a little practice. The basic steps are used over and over again in the various projects. The step-by-step diagrams and accompanying instructions are extremely easy to follow. The most difficult object to make in the book is the crane, but it is also the most fun. In

Japan, the crane is a symbol of good luck and can be found, in some form or other, practically any place—in the textile designs on women's kimonos, hung from the ceilings of temples and shrines as offereings from the people who go there to pray, or strung on pieces of thread to decorate a room.

It is easy to think of ways in which to use objects folded from paper. A few ideas are given at the back of this book, especially for parties and games. Origami figures can also be used as the background for plays, in sand table displays, and as murals in classrooms.

Here are some tips for those who are just beginning to try their hand at origami:

1. All of the objects illustrated in this book are made by folding perfectly squares pieces of paper. At first, five- or six-inch squares are the easiest to work with. Use thin paper, not heavy construction or art paper.

2. You must follow the directions step by step. Proper shapes can only be only be obtained through careful, symmetrical foldings.

3. If the figures seem too complicated, practice first by making marks on the corners of your paper to correspond with those in the diagrams.

4. It is a good idea to practice making an object with ordinary paper first so as not to waste colored paper.

5. For a delightful mixed color effect, two sheets of different colors may be used by placing them back to back and folding them simultaneously.

FLORENCE SAKADE

DOLLS

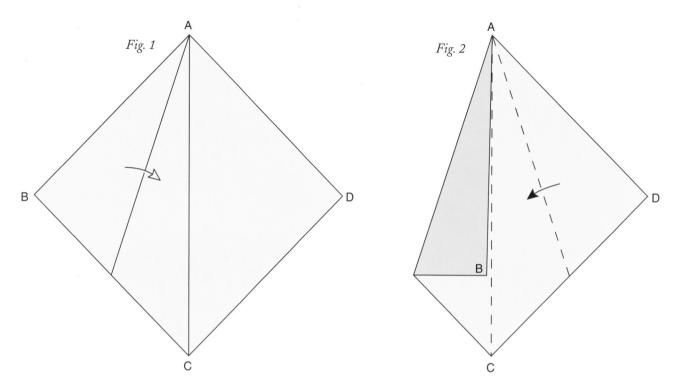

Step 1. Fold a square piece of paper (Fig. 1) so that the edge AB extends over as far as the center line AC as shown in Fig. 2.

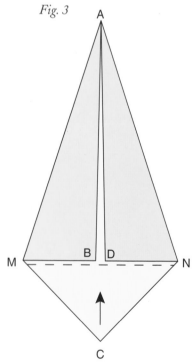

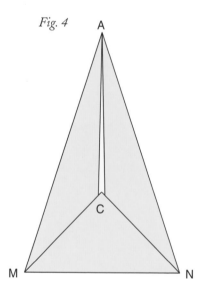

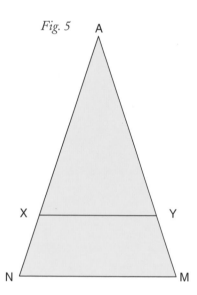

Step 2. Do the same with AD in order to get Fig. 3.

Step 3. Fold along MN so that point C is over and above points B and D. See Fig. 4.

Step 4. Turn the paper over and fold back MN along XY about two-fifths of the way up (Fig. 5) to get Fig. 6.

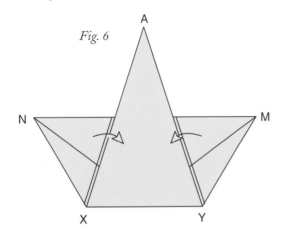

Fig. 6

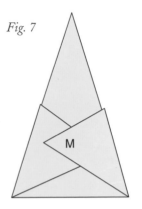

Fig. 7

Step 5. Fold points M and N forward along AY and AX so as to overlap each other, as in Fig. 7.

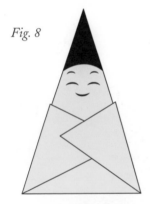

Fig. 8

Step 6. Complete the doll by drawing the face (Fig. 8).

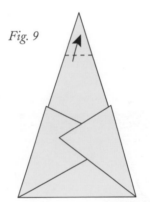

Fig. 9

Fig. 10

Step 7. To make a princess (Fig. 10), fold back the top of the head as shown in Fig. 9.

FAN

Fig. 1

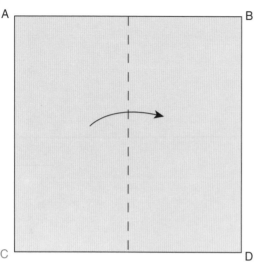

Step 1. Take a square piece of paper and fold it in half (Fig. 1). Make lengthwise folds (accordion fashion) across the entire breadth of the paper (Fig. 2) and then open it up to get Fig. 3.

Fig. 2

Fig. 3

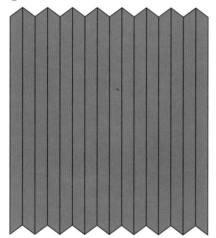

Step 2. Fold in half as shown in Fig. 4 and paste the center pleats together.

Fig. 4

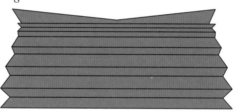

Step 3. To complete the fan, tie a piece of string or wool about half an inch up from the bottom (see photograph).

SAILBOAT

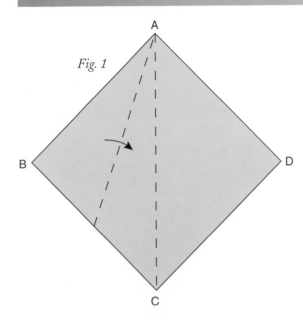

Fig. 1

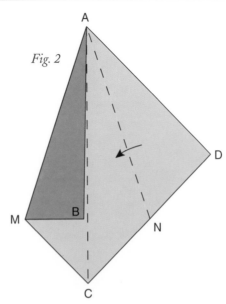

Fig. 2

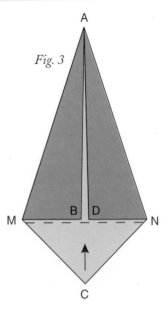

Fig. 3

Step 1. Take a square piece of paper and fold it along line AC so that point B meets point D. Fold and then reopen as in Fig. 1.

Step 2. Fold AB over to meet the center line AC (Fig. 2).

Step 3. Do the same with AD so as to make Fig. 3.

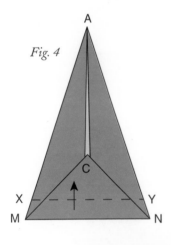

Fig. 4

Step 4. Fold along line MN as that point C is above points B and D. See Fig. 4.

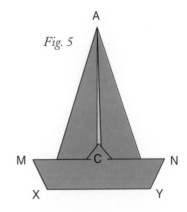

Fig. 5

Step 5. To complete the sailboat, fold along line XY so that points M and N appear as in Fig. 5.

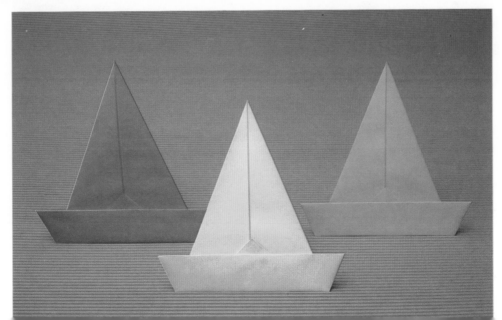

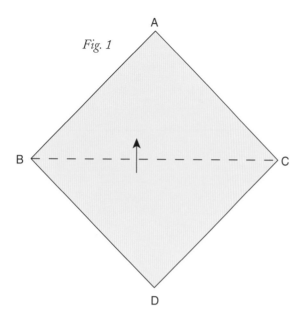

Fig. 1

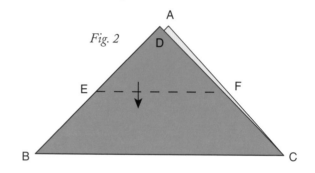

Fig. 2

Step 1. Fold a square piece of paper (Fig. 1) at BC so that point D is over point A, resulting in Fig. 2.

Step 2. Fold at EF so that point D is brought forward to touch line BC at the center, as shown in Fig. 3.

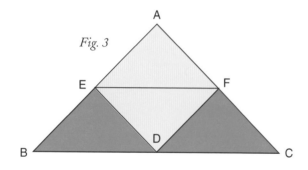

Fig. 3

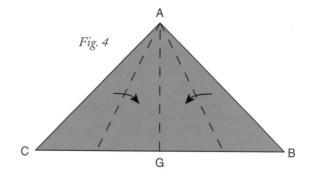

Fig. 4

Step 3. Turn the paper over as in Fig. 4. Bring AC forward until it is lined up on the center line AG. Do the same with AB. The result will be Fig. 5.

Step 4. Bring point M forward and fold on the dotted line shown in Fig. 5 so that M touches line AC. Do the same with point N and you will have Fig. 6.

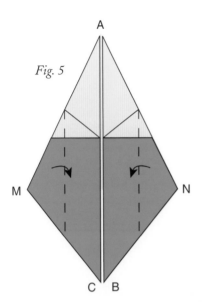

Fig. 5

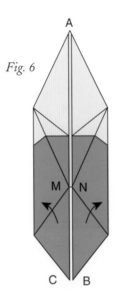

Fig. 6

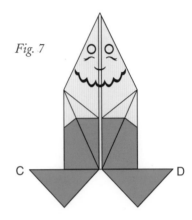

Fig. 7

Step 6. To complete, draw in Santa's face.

Step 5. Lift up point C and fold it over to the left as shown in Fig. 7. Do the same with point B, folding it over to the right.

CHRISTMAS TREE

Fig. 1

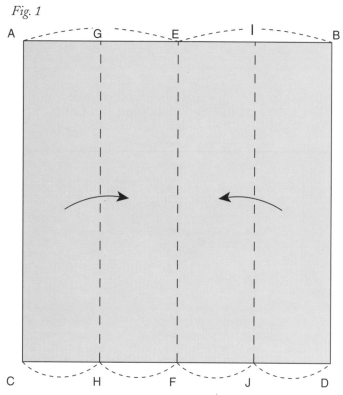

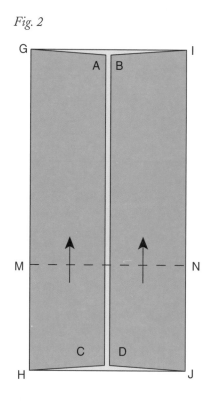

Step 1. Take a square piece of paper and fold at GH and at IJ (Fig. 1) so that edges AC and BD meet at the center, EF, as in Fig. 2.

Step 2. Fold at MN, about two-fifths of the way up, so that the edge HI appears as in Fig. 3.

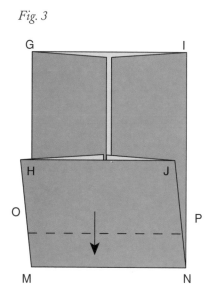

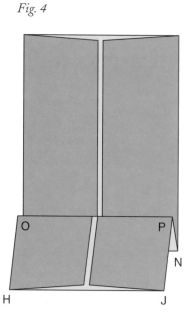

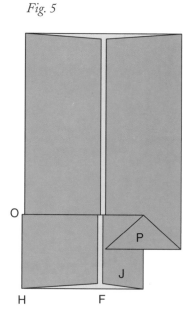

Step 3. Fold at OP so that point HJ appears as in Fig. 4.

Step 4. Fold point J over to the left so that it is above F, as shown in Fig. 5. Note that in doing so, point P is raised toward you and opened up so that it is in a new position and is no longer a corner. Do the same with H to get Fig. 6.

Step 5. Fold along EM bringing point G forward.

Fig. 6

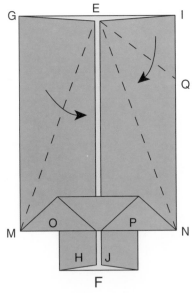

Step 6. Fold the corner I forward at EQ so that it touches EN.

Fig. 7

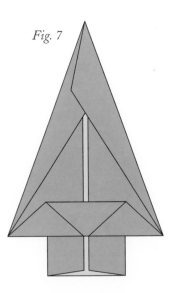

Step 7. Fold along EN bringing point Q forward. The result is shown in Fig. 7.

Fig. 8

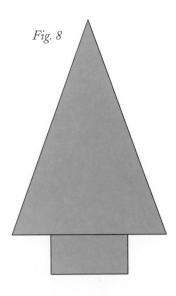

Step 8. Turn the paper over and decorate the Christmas tree with color pens or pieces of shiny paper.

FLOWERS

Fig. 1

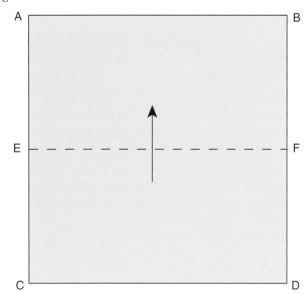

Step 1. Fold a square piece of paper in the
middle (Fig. 1) at EF in order to get Fig. 2.

Fig. 2

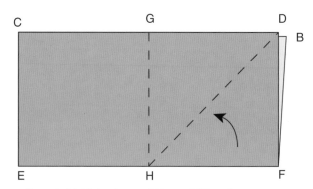

Step 2. Fold in the middle at GH and reopen.

Fig. 3

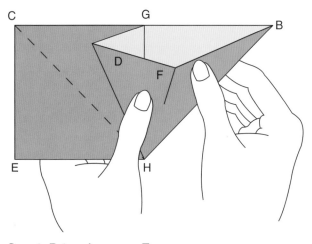

Step 3. Bring the corner F up
between D and B so that it meets
G, thus placing HF along GH.
See Fig. 3. DHB will then form
an upside-down triangle.

Fig. 4

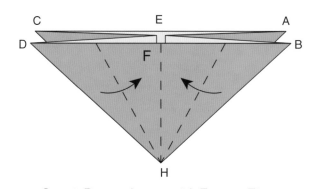

Step 4. Repeat the step with E to get Fig. 4.

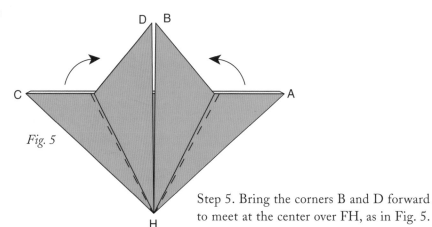

Fig. 5

Step 5. Bring the corners B and D forward
to meet at the center over FH, as in Fig. 5.

Fig. 6

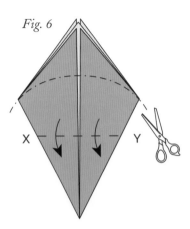

Step 6. Turn the paper over and do the same with A and C.

Fig. 7

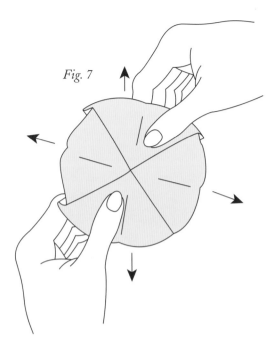

Step 7. Cut off the points with a pair of scissors, as shown in Fig. 6.

Fig. 8

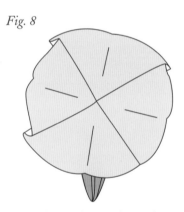

Step 8. Open the petals, as shown in Fig. 7, as far down as XY and you will get Fig. 8.

Fig. 9

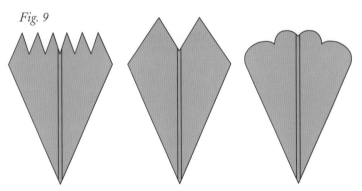

Step 9. It is possible to make different kinds of flowers by cutting the petals into various shapes. See Fig. 9.

CUP

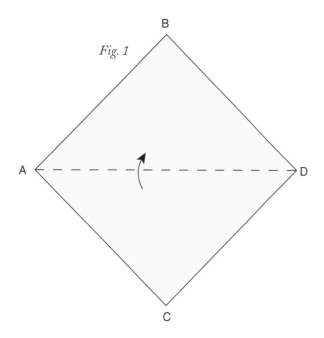

Fig. 1

Step 1. Fold a square piece of paper along line AD (Fig. 1) so that point C is on top of point B, as in Fig. 2.

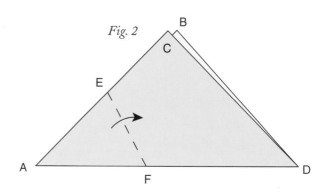

Fig. 2

Step 2. Fold at EF so that point A extends over to the edge CD at point G, and so that EG is parallel to FD, as in Fig. 3.

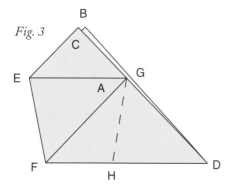

Fig. 3

Step 3. Do the same thing with point D so that DG is on top of EA, as in Fig. 4.

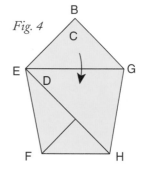

Fig. 4

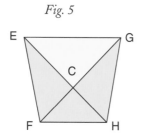

Fig. 5

Step 4. Finish the cup by separating points C and B, folding point C forward along EG and folding point B in the opposite direction along EG. The finished cup is shown in Fig. 5.

HOUSE

Fig. 1

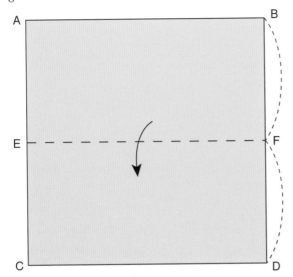

Step 1. Fold a square piece of paper at EF (Fig. 1) so that edge AB is on top of edge CD, as in Fig. 2.

Fig. 2

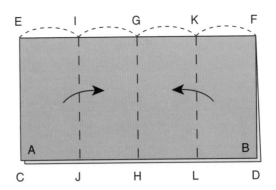

Step 2. Fold the edges AEC and BDF forward so that they meet at the center line GH, as shown in Fig. 3.

Fig. 3

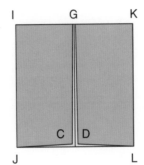

Step 3. Separate points B and D by holding B in place and swinging point D over to the right, thus bringing point F to the position shown in Fig. 4.

Fig. 4

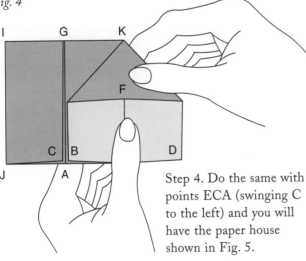

Step 4. Do the same with points ECA (swinging C to the left) and you will have the paper house shown in Fig. 5.

Fig. 5

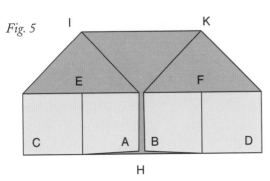

Step 5. Complete the house by drawing in the windows.

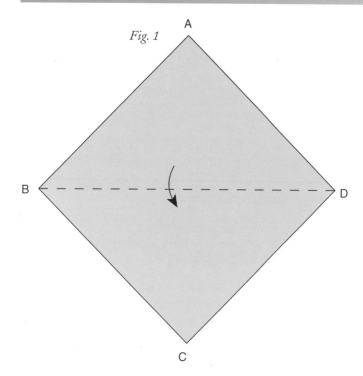

Fig. 1

Step 1. Fold a square piece of paper along line BD (Fig. 1) so that corner A is over corner C, as shown in Fig. 2.

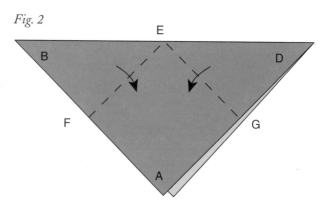

Fig. 2

Step 2. Fold along EF and EG so that corners B and D meet at point A, as in Fig. 3.

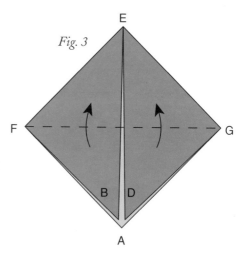

Fig. 3

Step 3. Fold up points B and D so that they meet at E, as shown in Fig. 4.

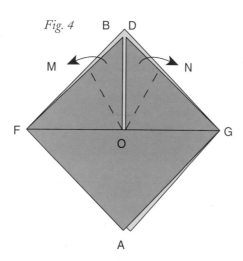

Fig. 4

Step 4. Bring forward point B and fold this flap along OM, as shown in Fig. 5. Point M is about one-third of the way down EF.

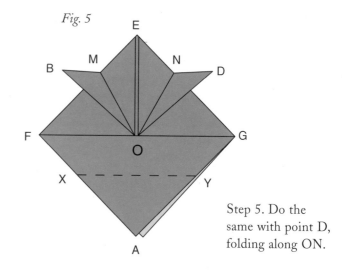

Fig. 5

Step 5. Do the same with point D, folding along ON.

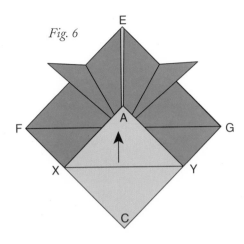

Fig. 6

Step 6. Fold at XY (Fig. 6) so that A is over and above point O.

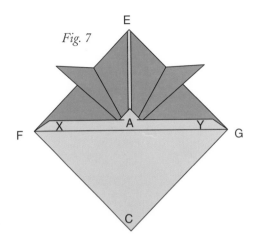

Fig. 7

Step 7. Fold this front flap again at FG, making Fig. 7.

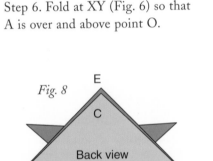

Fig. 8

Back view

Step 8. Turn over and fold C so that it meets E (Fig. 8).

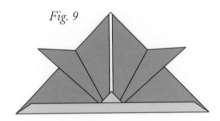

Fig. 9

Step 9. Turn over again and you have Fig. 9.

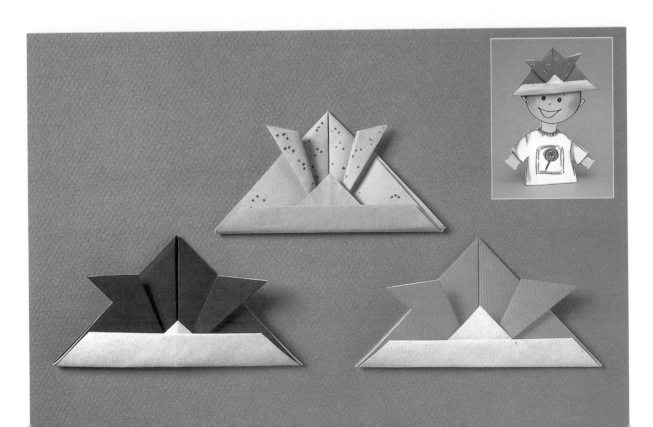

Fig. 1

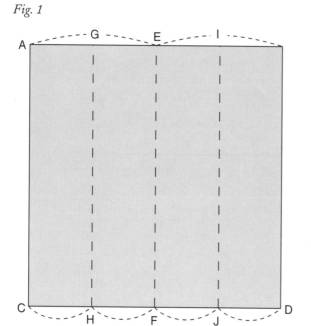

Step 1. Fold a square piece of paper down the center on line EF, as shown in Fig. 1, crease, and then unfold.

Fig. 2

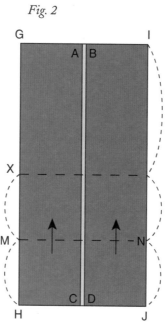

Step 2. Fold at GH and IJ so that edges AC and BD meet at the center line EF. This results in Fig. 2.

Fig. 3

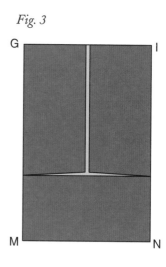

Step 3. Fold at MN so that edge HJ reaches the center line XY, thus forming Fig. 3.

Fig. 4

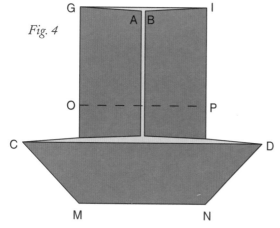

Step 4. Pull out corners C and D in order to form Fig. 4.

Fig. 5

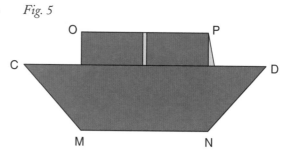

Step 5. Fold backwards at OP so that the edge GI is directly under MN, as shown in Fig. 5.

Fig. 6

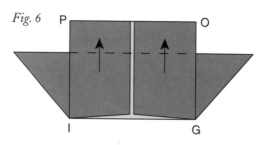

Step 6. Turn over to get Fig. 6.

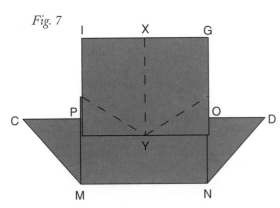

Fig. 7

Step 7. Fold so that the edge IG is over and above PO, as shown in Fig. 7.

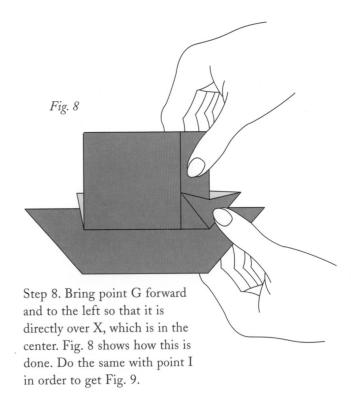

Fig. 8

Step 8. Bring point G forward and to the left so that it is directly over X, which is in the center. Fig. 8 shows how this is done. Do the same with point I in order to get Fig. 9.

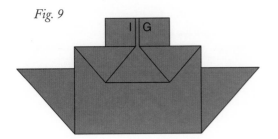

Fig. 9

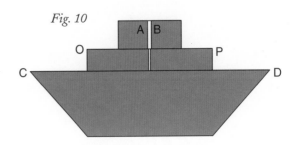

Fig. 10

Step 9. Turn over and you have the ship shown in Fig. 10. Draw portholes on the sides (see photograph).

LANTERN

Fig. 1

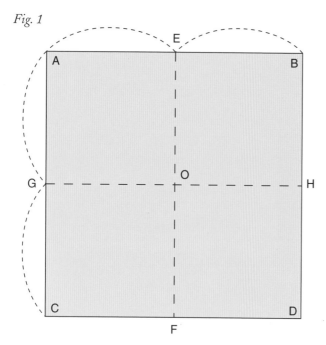

Step 1. Fold a square piece of paper, as shown in Fig. 1, and then spread open.

Fig. 2

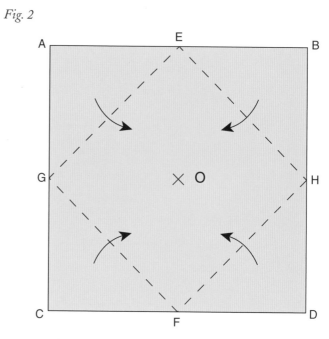

Step 2. Fold the four corners A, B, C and D forward so that they meet at the center, as in Figs. 2 and 3.

Fig. 3

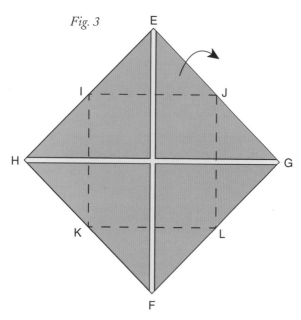

Step 3. Turn over and fold the four corners E, F, G and H so that they meet at the center, as in Fig. 4.

Fig. 4

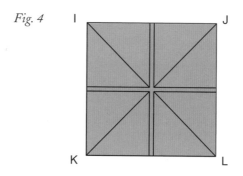

Step 4. Turn the paper over once more and you will have Fig. 5.

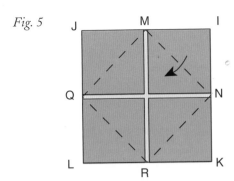

Fig. 5

Step 5. Next, fold the corners I, J, K and L forward once more to meet at the center. Turn the paper and you will have Fig. 6.

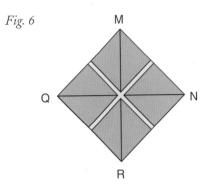

Fig. 6

Step 6. Using both thumbs, push open MZ, as in Figs. 7 and 8. Do the same with ZR and you will get Fig. 9.

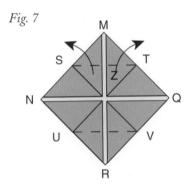

Fig. 7

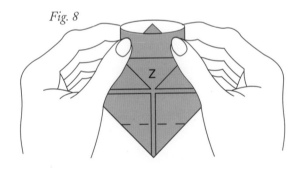

Fig. 8

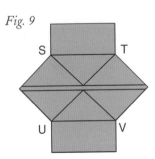

Fig. 9

Step 7. Hang the lantern with a bamboo skewer and thread.

23

FISH

Fig. 1

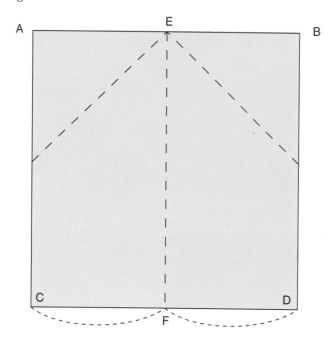

Step 1. Fold a square piece of paper down the center at EF, as shown in Fig. 1, crease, and then unfold.

Fig. 2

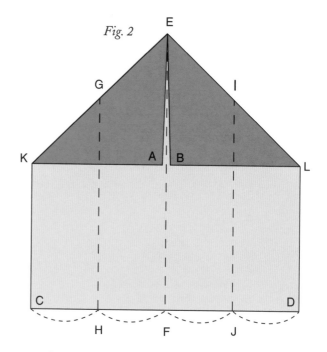

Step 2. Bring forward corners A and B until they meet along the center line EF, forming Fig. 2.

Fig. 3

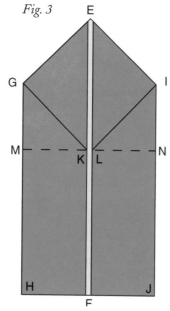

Step 3. Fold at GH and IJ so that the edges KC and LD meet at the center line EF, as shown in Fig. 3.

Fig. 4

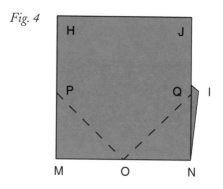

Step 4. Fold upward at MN so that HJ meets point E as in Fig. 4.

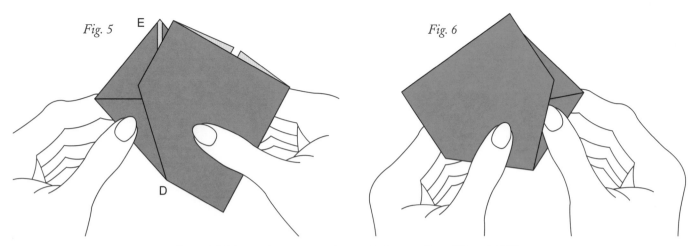

Fig. 5

Fig. 6

Step 5. Pick up the paper and spread the two flaps HJ and GEI so that point M can be pushed up between them and extended as far as the center line EF. See Figs. 4, 5 and 6. Do the same with point N. The result will be Fig. 7.

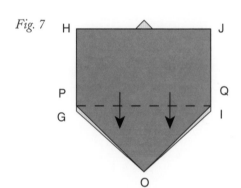

Fig. 7

Step 6. Fold down the front flap at PQ in order to get Fig. 8.

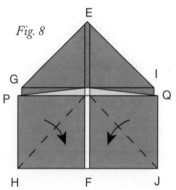

Fig. 8

Step 7. Bend forward points P and Q so that they meet at F (Fig. 9).

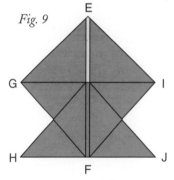

Fig. 9

Step 8. Turn over and draw an eye, as in Fig. 10.

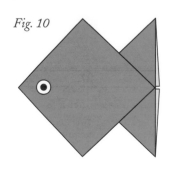

Fig. 10

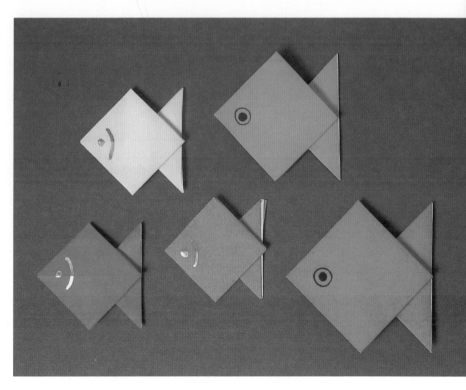

WINDMILL

Fig. 1

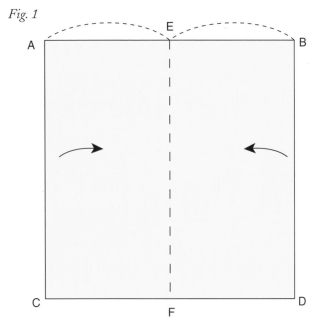

Step 1. Take a square piece of paper and fold it so that AC and BD (Fig. 1) meet at the center line EF and look like Fig. 2.

Fig. 2

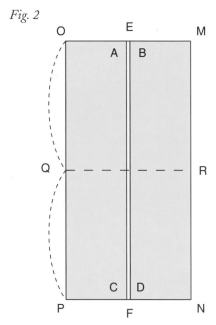

Step 2. Fold OM back along the line QR so that OM meets PN. This will result in Fig. 3.

Fig. 3

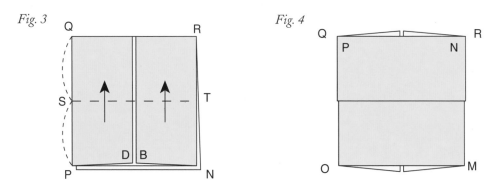

Fig. 4

Step 3. Fold along ST so that PN meets QR, as in Fig. 4. Note that flap OM remains where it is for the present.

Fig. 5

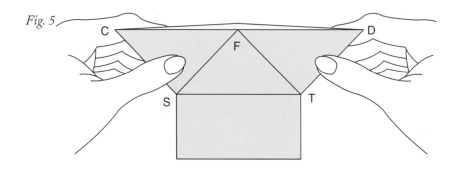

Step 4. Pull out corners D and C, as in Fig. 5.

Fig. 6

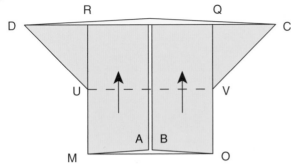

Step 5. Turn the paper over and fold so that MO meets RQ (Fig. 6). Pull out corners A and B and you will get Fig. 7.

Fig. 7

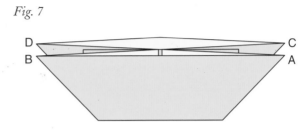

Step 6. Spread out Fig. 7 so that it looks like Fig. 8.

Fig. 8

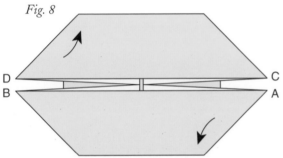

Step 7. Fold corner D upward and corner A downward and you will get Fig. 9.

Fig. 9

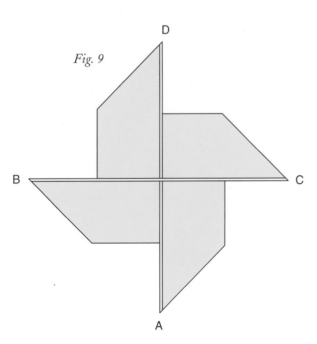

Step 8. Secure the windmill to a straw with a pin (see photograph).

SWAN

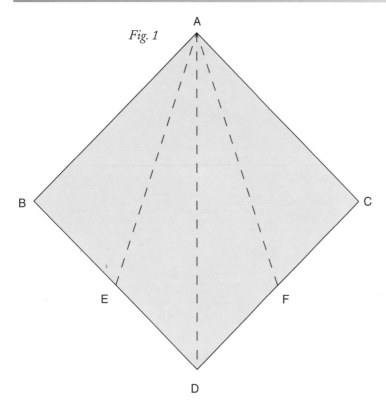

Fig. 1

Step 1. Fold a square piece of paper along line AD (Fig. 1) and then unfold.

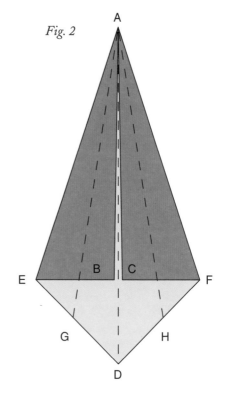

Fig. 2

Step 2. Fold the edge AB forward to meet the center line AD. Do the same with the edge AC and you will have Fig. 2.

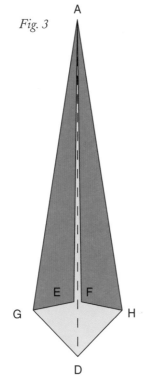

Fig. 3

Step 3. Now fold the edge AE forward so that it reaches the center line AD, and then repeat with edge AF. You now have Fig. 3.

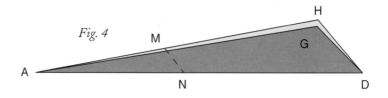

Fig. 4

Step 4. Fold along the center line AD so that AG is on top of AH, as in Fig. 4.

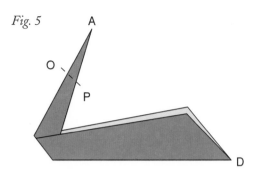

Fig. 5

Step 5. To make the neck, pick up the paper with the open edge at the top and with corner A pointing to the left. Separate the two flaps slightly and bend back the pointed end at MN, as in Fig. 5, so that it is inserted between the body flaps. In doing so, the fold along the line AD in the neck portion will be reversed.

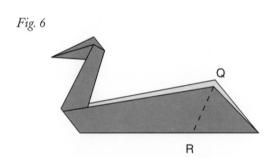

Fig. 6

Step 6. The head is formed in a similar way at OP. See Fig. 6.

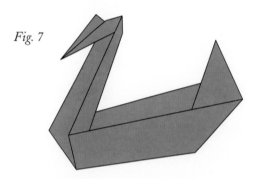

Fig. 7

Step 7. The tail is formed at QR (Figs. 6 and 7) in the same way as the neck and head. Follow the diagrams carefully to get the proper angles for the neck, head and tail.

Fig. 1

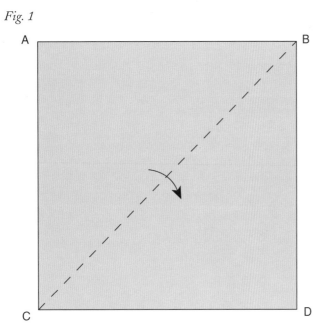

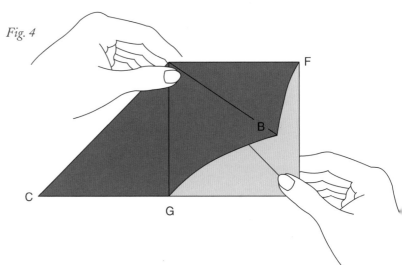

Fig. 2

Step 1. Fold a square piece of paper at BC (Fig. 1) so that point A is over point D, as shown in Fig. 2.

Step 2. Fold at ED so that point B is over point C, resulting in Fig. 3.

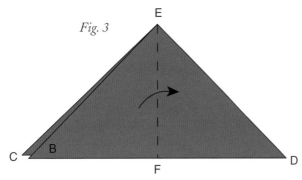

Fig. 3

Step 3. As shown in Figs. 3 and 4, open B and bring it over until it is directly above D. Crease the paper along EF and EG.

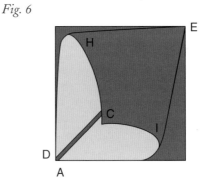

Fig. 5

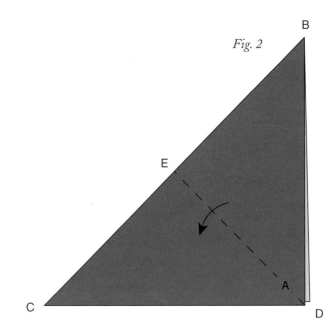

Fig. 6

Step 4. Turn it over and you will have Fig. 5. Do the same with C as you did with B, and the result will be Fig. 6.

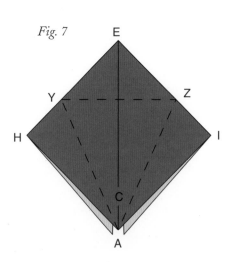

Fig. 7

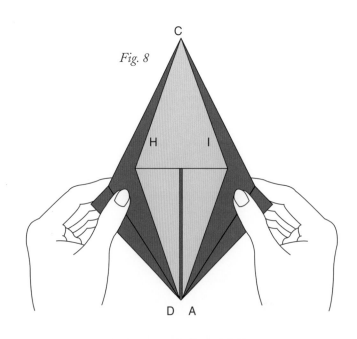

Fig. 8

Step 5. Crease at YC and ZC (Fig. 7) so that points H and I meet along line EC, and then unfold.

Step 6. Lift up C and fold at YZ so that H and I meet at the middle along line AC. Fig. 8 shows this step being executed and Fig. 9 shows it completed.

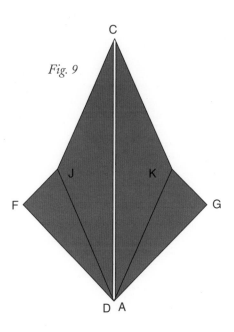

Fig. 9

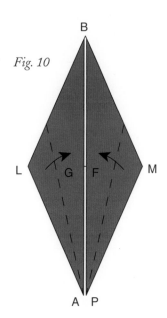

Fig. 10

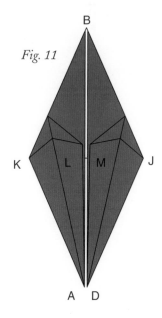

Fig. 11

Step 7. Turn the paper over and repeat Steps 5 and 6. The result will be Fig. 10.

Step 8. Fold on the dotted line shown in Fig. 10 so that L and M meet at the middle along lines BA and BD, as shown in Fig. 11.

Step 9. Turn the paper over and fold J and K the same way you did L and M. The result is shown in Fig. 12.

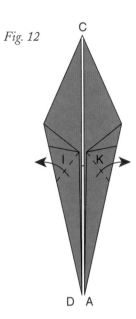

Fig. 12

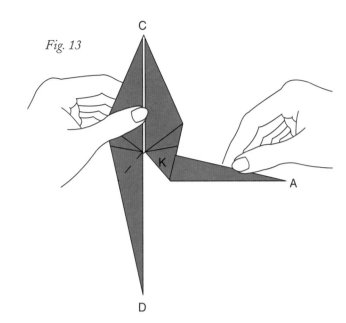

Fig. 13

Step 10. Lift A up toward the right, as shown in Fig. 13 and fold at K. In doing so, reverse the fold down the middle of this flap, thus forming the neck.

Step 11. Next make the head and then fold D to the left to make the tail. The head, neck and tail are made in the same way as those of the "Swan" (see page 29, Figs. 5, 6 and 7).

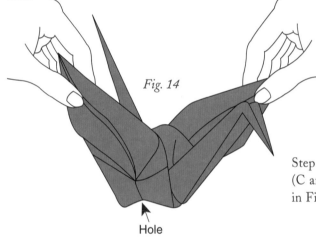

Fig. 14

Hole

Step 12. To complete the crane, spread the wings (C and B) open and blow through the hole indicated in Fig. 14 in order to swell out the body.

DOG

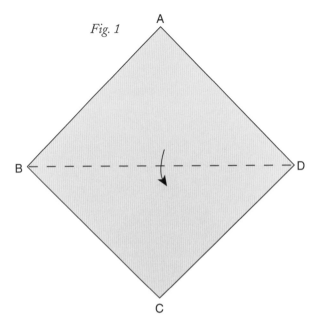

Fig. 1

Step 1. Fold a square piece of paper along line BD (Fig. 1) so that corner A falls on corner C (Fig. 2).

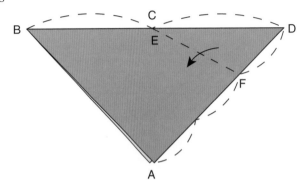

Fig. 2

Step 2. Fold along EF (Fig. 2), bringing corner D forward (Fig. 3). Point F is one-third of the way down DA (Fig. 2).

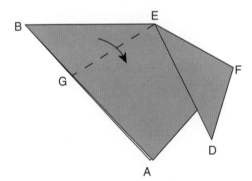

Fig. 3

Step 3. Repeat Step 2 on the other side at EG (Figs. 3 and 4).

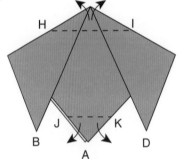

Fig. 4

Step 4. Fold back along HI and JK (Figs. 4 and 5).

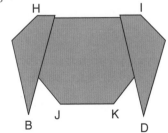

Fig. 5

Step 5. Complete the dog by drawing the face.

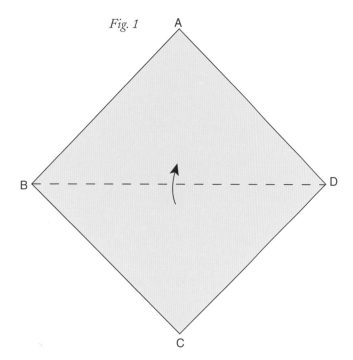

Fig. 1

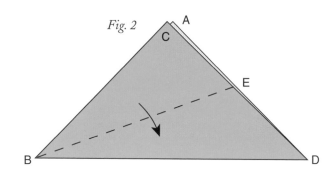

Fig. 2

Step 1. Fold a square piece of paper along line BD (Fig. 1) so that corner C falls on corner A (Fig. 2).

Step 2. Create BE by bringing BC and BA down to fall on BD (Figs. 2 and 3).

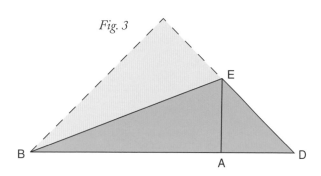

Fig. 3

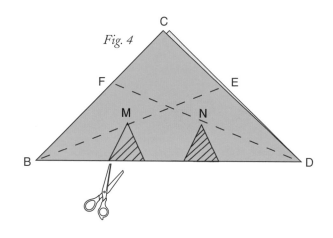

Fig. 4

Step 3. Make another crease as in Step 2 along FD. Then cut out two triangles at M and N (Fig. 4).

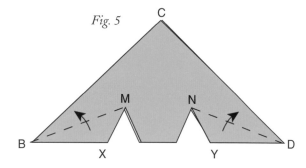

Fig. 5

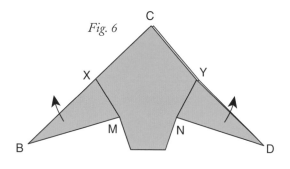

Fig. 6

Step 4. Fold along BM and DN (Fig. 5) so that X and Y fall on BC and DC respectively (Fig. 6).

Step 5. Fold corners B and D upward (Fig. 6) so that BM and DN are about vertical (Fig. 7).

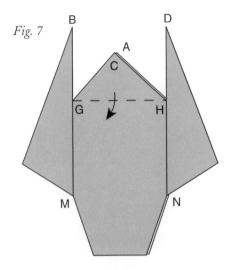

Fig. 7

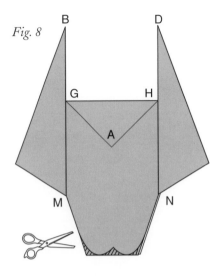

Fig. 8

Step 6. Fold along GH (Fig. 7), bringing corners C and A forward (Fig. 8).

Step 7. Turn the paper over, draw the face, and cut out the mouth.

PEACOCK

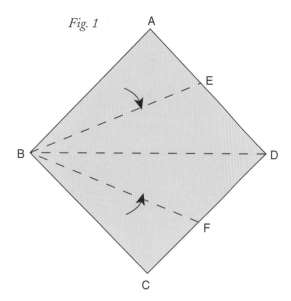

Fig. 1

Step 1. Fold a square piece of paper along lines BE and BF (Fig. 1) so that edges BA and BC meet at the center BD (Fig. 2).

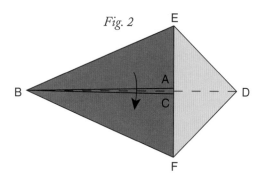

Fig. 2

Step 2. Fold along BD (Fig. 2) so that E falls on F (Fig. 3).

Fig. 3

Step 3. Fold back point B along MN (Figs. 3 and 4).

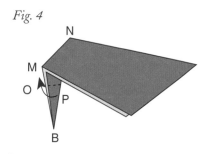

Fig. 4

Step 4. Fold along OP, bringing point B back and upward (Figs. 4 and 5).

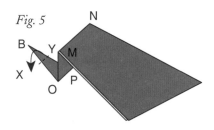

Fig. 5

Step 5. Make the head by folding along XY, turning point B back and downward to the left (Fig. 5).

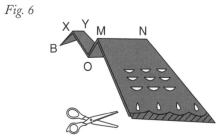

Fig. 6

Step 6. Draw the feathers and cut their ends (Fig. 6).

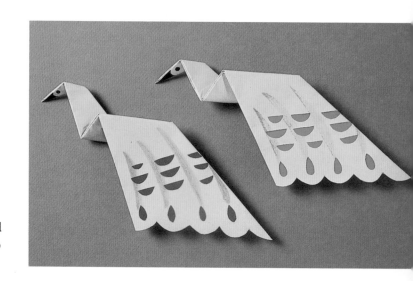

Note: By using two papers of different colors, one placed on top of the other, the feathers can be cut from the top paper and the other color will show from the inside.

PEAHEN

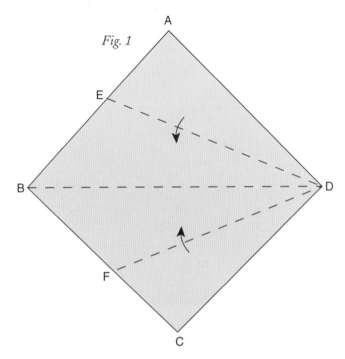

Fig. 1

Step 1. Fold a square piece of paper along lines DE and DF (Fig. 1) so that edges AD and CD meet at the center BD (Fig. 2).

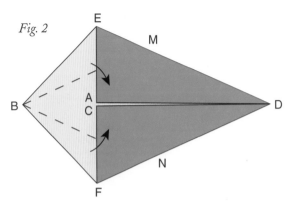

Fig. 2

Step 2. Fold along BM and BN (Fig. 2) so that BE and BF meet at BD (Fig. 3).

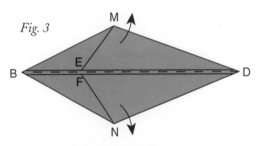

Fig. 3

Step 3. Fold in half outward along BD (Figs. 3 and 4).

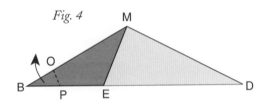

Fig. 4

Step 4. Fold back point B along OP (Figs. 4 and 5).

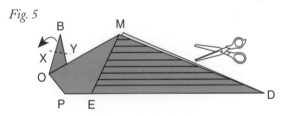

Fig. 5

Step 5. Make the head by folding along XY, turning point B downward to the left (Figs. 5 and 6).

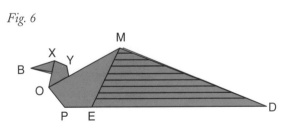

Fig. 6

Step 6. Cut lines parallel to ED to make the feathers (Figs. 5 and 6).

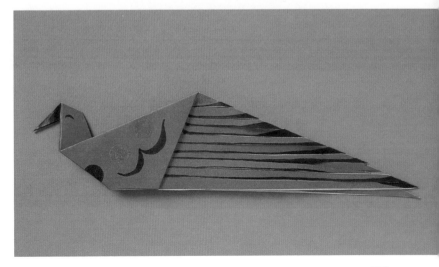

GIRAFFE

Fig. 1

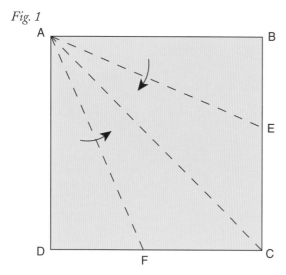

Fig. 2

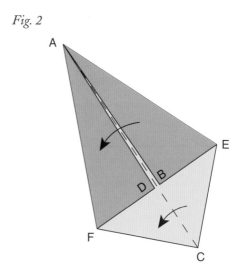

Step 1. Fold a square piece of paper along lines AE and AF (Fig. 1) so that edges AB and AD meet at the center AC (Fig. 2).

Step 2. Fold in half at AC (Fig. 2) so that AE falls on AF (Fig. 3).

Fig. 3

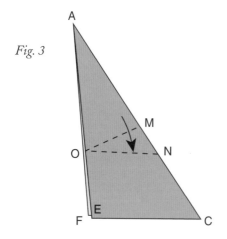

Fig. 4

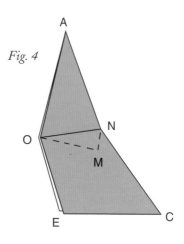

Step 3. Fold along OM and ON, inserting point M between the two body flaps. O is a little less than halfway down AE (Figs. 3 and 4).

Step 4. Fold in along AE (Fig. 5) so that point O is inside the body flap.

Fig. 5

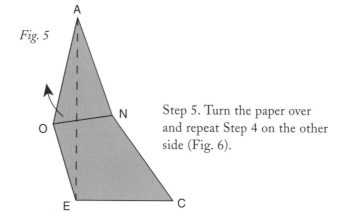

Step 5. Turn the paper over and repeat Step 4 on the other side (Fig. 6).

Fig. 6

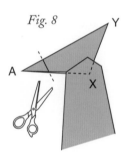

Step 6. Cut out the legs (Fig. 7), make slit XY on the back of the neck to make the head and ears (Figs. 7 and 8), cut off A (Fig. 8), and draw the eyes and spots on the body.

Fig. 7

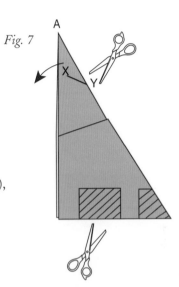

Fig. 8

ELEPHANT

Fig. 1

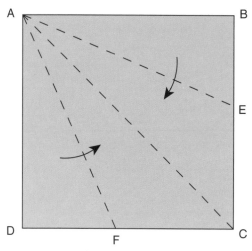

Step 1. Fold a square piece of paper along lines AE and AF (Fig. 1) so that edges AB and AD meet at the center AC (Fig. 2).

Fig. 2

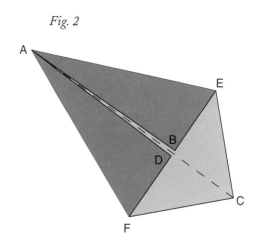

Step 2. Fold along AC (Fig. 2) so that corner E falls on corner F (Fig. 3).

Fig. 3

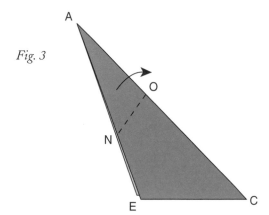

Step 3. Fold along ON (Fig. 3), bringing point A forward and across to the right so that NA is about parallel to EC (Fig. 4).

Fig. 4

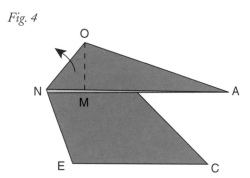

Step 4. Lift the top flap at M (Fig. 4) and open corner O, bringing point A across to the left so that OA falls almost on ON (Fig. 5).

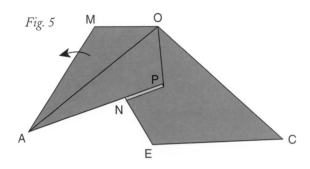

Fig. 5

Step 5. Fold back point M along OA (Figs. 5 and 6).

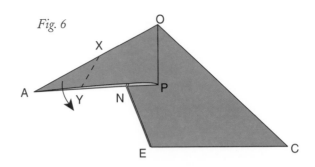

Fig. 6

Step 6. Crease XY (Fig. 6), separate the two flaps of the ears, and bring point A down between the flaps (Fig. 7).

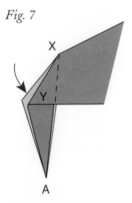

Fig. 7

Step 7. Draw the eyes and cut out the legs and tail (Fig. 8). Add white paper for the tusks (see photograph).

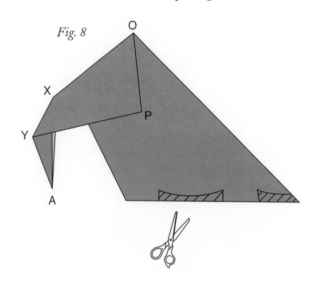

Fig. 8

Fig. 1

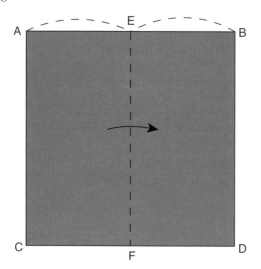

Step 1. Fold a square piece of paper along line EF (Fig. 1) so that AC falls on BD (Fig. 2).

Fig. 2

Step 2. Fold forward at GH, about one-quarter of an inch down from EA, and once more at IJ (Figs. 2 and 3).

Fig. 3

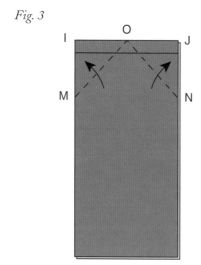

Step 3. Fold back corners I and J along OM and ON (Fig. 3) so that OI and OJ meet at the center in the back (Fig. 4). Point O is halfway between I and J.

Fig. 4

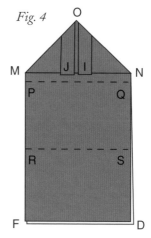

Step 4. Fold back point O along PQ, and then fold forward along RS so that PQ falls on FD (Figs. 4 and 5).

Fig. 5

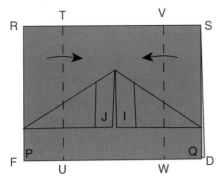

Step 5. Fold along TU and VW (Fig. 5) so that RF and SD touch the collar lines J and I respectively (Fig. 6).

Fig. 6

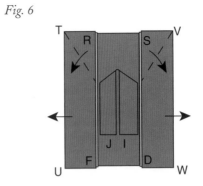

Step 6. Lift F, separating it from P, and open corner R so that point R falls on TU. Do the same with D and S (Figs. 6 and 7).

Fig. 7

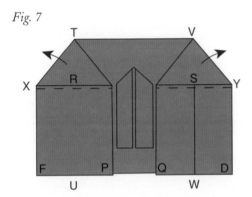

Step 7. Fold back along XY (Figs. 7 and 8).

Fig. 8

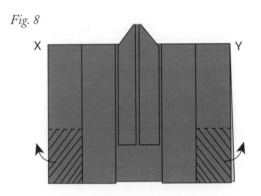

Step 8. To make the sleeves, fold back flap (Fig. 8).

Note: An oblong piece of paper or cloth about three times as long as it is wide can be used as well to make this kimono. In that case, Step 1 would be omitted.

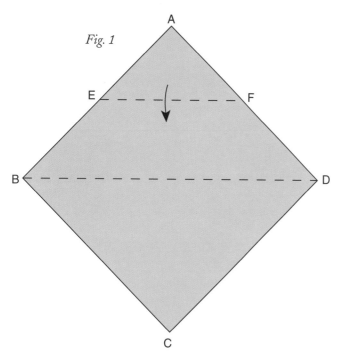

Step 1. Fold a square piece of paper along line EF (Fig. 1) so that corner A touches BD at the center (Fig. 2).

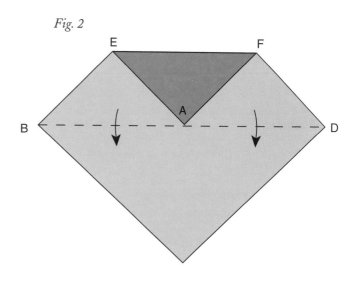

Step 2. Fold forward along BD (Figs. 2 and 3).

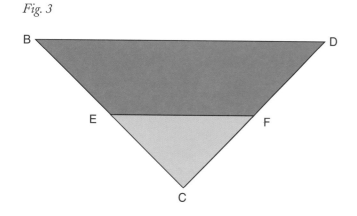

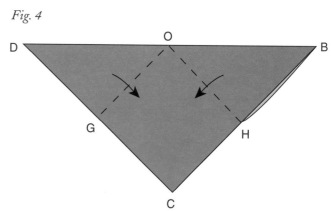

Step 3. Turn the paper over and fold along OG and OH (Fig. 4), bringing corners D and B forward to meet at C (Fig. 5).

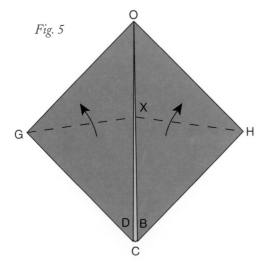

Fig. 5

Step 4. Fold along XG and XH (Fig. 5), bringing corners D and B up, but off O (Fig. 6). Point X then is not on GH but a little higher up on CO.

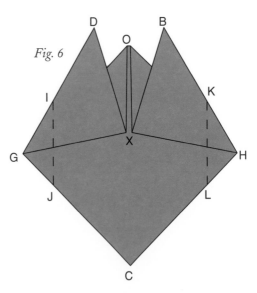

Fig. 6

Step 5. Fold along IJ and KL (Fig. 6) so that points G and H come forward on GH (Fig. 7).

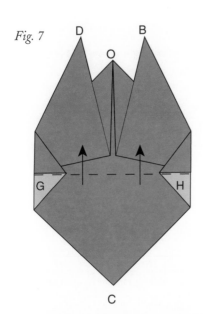

Fig. 7

Step 6. Fold along GH (Fig. 7) so that corner C falls on O (Fig. 8).

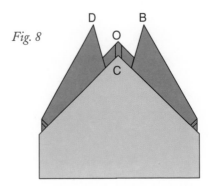

Fig. 8

Step 7. Turn the paper over and draw the face and ears.

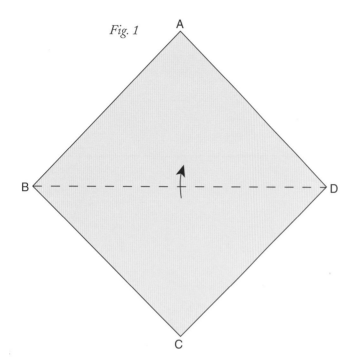

Fig. 1

Step 1. Fold a square piece of paper along line BD (Fig. 1) so that corner C falls on corner A (Fig. 2).

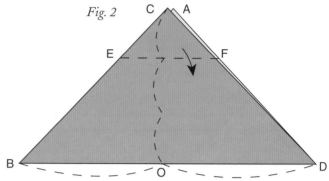

Fig. 2

Step 2. Fold along EF (Fig. 2), bringing corners C and A forward (Fig. 3). EF is about one-third of the way down CO (Fig. 2).

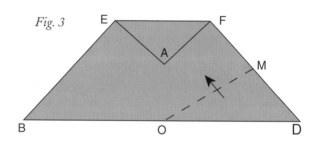

Fig. 3

Step 3. Fold along OM (Fig. 3), bringing corner D up so that OD meets F (Fig. 4).

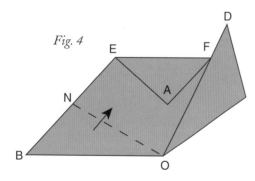

Fig. 4

Step 4. Repeat Step 3 on the other side at ON (Figs. 4 and 5).

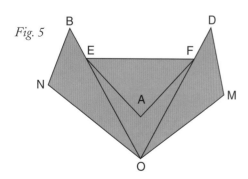

Fig. 5

Step 5. Turn the paper over and draw the face.

CLOWN

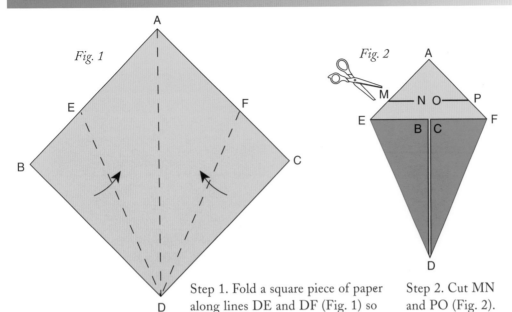

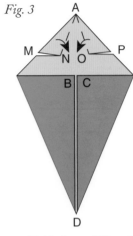

Fig. 1

Fig. 2

Fig. 3

Step 1. Fold a square piece of paper along lines DE and DF (Fig. 1) so that edges BD and CD meet at the center AD (Fig. 2).

Step 2. Cut MN and PO (Fig. 2).

Step 3. Fold along AN and AO (Fig. 3) so that the two side flaps overlap each other (Fig. 4).

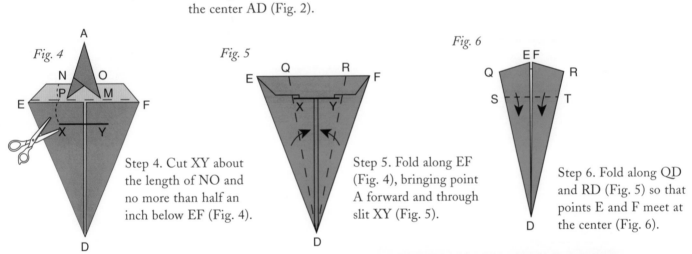

Fig. 4

Fig. 5

Fig. 6

Step 4. Cut XY about the length of NO and no more than half an inch below EF (Fig. 4).

Step 5. Fold along EF (Fig. 4), bringing point A forward and through slit XY (Fig. 5).

Step 6. Fold along QD and RD (Fig. 5) so that points E and F meet at the center (Fig. 6).

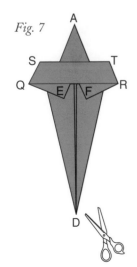

Fig. 7

Step 7. Fold along ST (Fig. 6), bringing QR forward. Point A will come up by itself (Fig. 7). Line ST is on XY. To make the legs, cut the lower part of AD from D. Turn the paper over and draw the face and costume.

FOX

Fig. 1

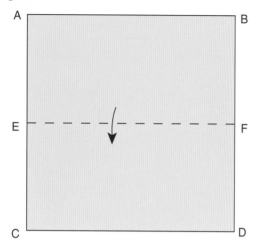

Step 1. Fold a square piece of paper along line EF (Fig. 1) so that AB falls on CD (Fig. 2).

Fig. 2

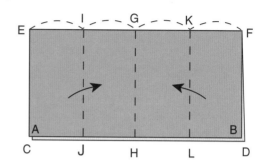

Step 2. Fold along IJ and KL (Fig. 2) so that edges AEG and BDF meet at center GH (Fig. 3).

Fig. 3

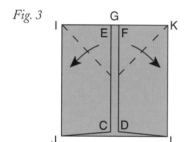

Step 3. Open corner F (Fig. 3) by lifting D toward the right while holding B in place (Fig. 4).

Fig. 4

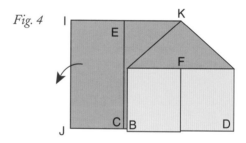

Step 4. Repeat Step 3 with ECA (Figs. 4 and 5) (see the "House" on page 17, Figs. 1–5) and turn the paper over (Fig. 6).

Fig. 5

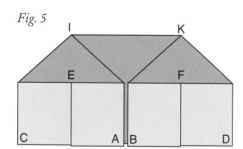

Fig. 6

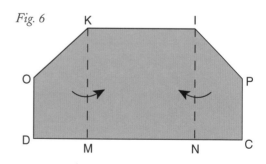

Step 5. Fold along KM and IN (Fig. 6) so that edges OD and PC meet at the center (Fig. 7).

Fig. 7

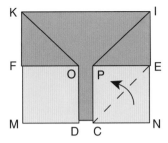

Step 6. Fold the top flap along EC (Fig. 7) so that N falls on P (Fig. 8).

Fig. 8

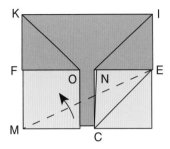

Step 7. Fold along EM (Figs. 8 and 9).

Fig. 9

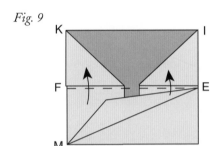

Step 8. Fold the top flap along FE (Fig. 9) so that point M falls on K (Fig. 10).

Fig. 10

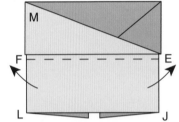

Step 9. Turn the paper over and repeat Steps 7, 8 and 9, but note that L is on the right-hand side while M is on the left (Fig. 11).

Step 10. Separate the two flaps by putting your thumb into I and index finger into K from the back under EF (Fig. 11). Push back the middle part of the face with the other hand, and the ears, L and M, will stand up (Fig. 12). Move the two fingers so that K and I meet.

Fig. 11

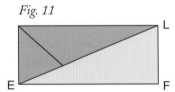

Fig. 12

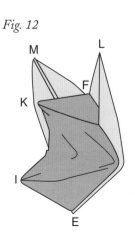

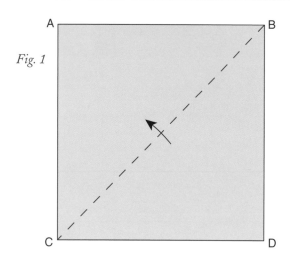

Fig. 1

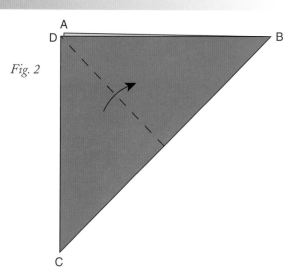

Fig. 2

Step 1. Fold a square piece of paper along line BC (Fig. 1) so that corner D falls on A (Fig. 2).

Step 2. Fold along ED (Fig. 2) so that point C falls on B (Fig. 3).

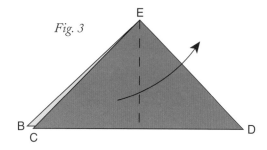

Fig. 3

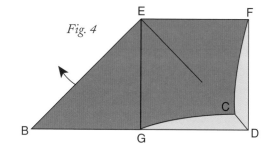

Fig. 4

Step 3. Open C (Fig. 3) and bring it over to the right, directly above D (Fig. 4). Place C on D and crease EF and EG (Fig. 4).

Step 4. Turn the paper over and repeat Step 3 with B (Figs. 4 and 5).

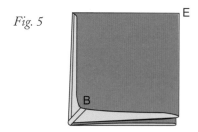

Fig. 5

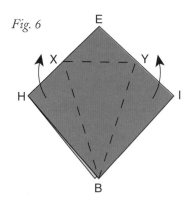

Fig. 6

Step 5. Crease at XB and YB (Fig. 6) so that HB and IB meet at EB.

Step 6. Lift up B and fold at XY (Fig. 6) so that H and I meet at the middle on BA and BD respectively (Figs. 7 and 8).

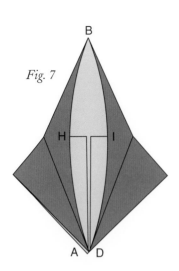

Fig. 7

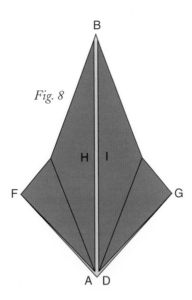

Fig. 8

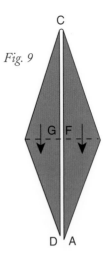

Fig. 9

Step 7. Turn the paper over and repeat Steps 5 and 6 (Fig. 9) (see the "Crane" on pages 30–31, Steps 1–10).

Step 8. Bring point C down on AD (Fig. 9), and do the same with B on the reverse side (Fig. 10).

Step 9. Fold in half along EB (Figs. 10 and 11). Then cut the top flap along CN, N being halfway up CE (Fig. 11).

Fig. 10

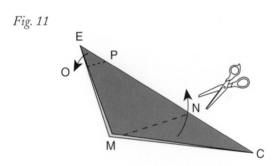

Fig. 11

Step 11. Turn the paper over and repeat Step 10 on the other side.

Step 10. Lift up C and fold along MN (Fig. 11) so that MN is about perpendicular to ME (Fig. 12).

Fig. 12

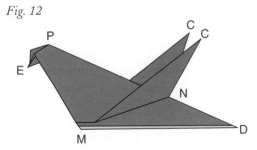

Step 12. Crease at OP (Fig. 11), separate the two body flaps, and bring point E down between the flaps (Fig. 12) (see the "Elephant" on page 41, Fig. 7).

CHURCH

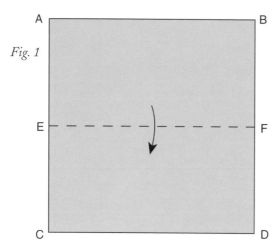

Fig. 1

Step 1. Fold a square piece of paper along line EF (Fig. 1) so that AB falls on CD (Fig. 2).

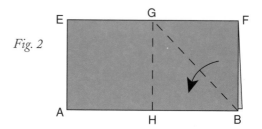

Fig. 2

Step 2. Crease in the middle at GH (Fig. 2).

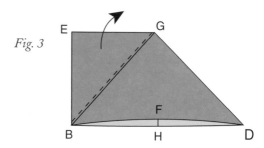

Fig. 3

Step 3. Open corner F (Fig. 2) and bring point F down between B and D so that GF falls on GH (Fig. 3). Crease GB and GD.

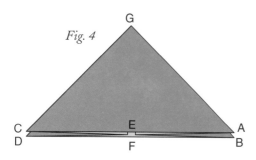

Fig. 4

Step 4. Turn the paper over and repeat Step 3 with E (Fig. 4) (see the "Flowers" on page 14, Figs. 1–4).

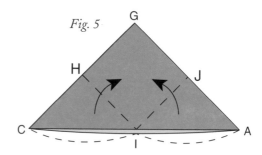

Fig. 5

Step 5. Fold along HI and JI (Fig. 5) so that points C and A meet at G (Fig. 6).

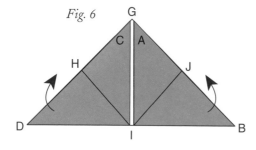

Fig. 6

Step 6. Turn the paper over and repeat Step 5 with B and D (Fig. 7).

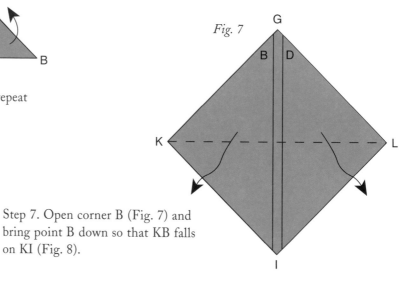

Fig. 7

Step 7. Open corner B (Fig. 7) and bring point B down so that KB falls on KI (Fig. 8).

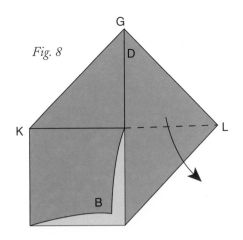

Fig. 8

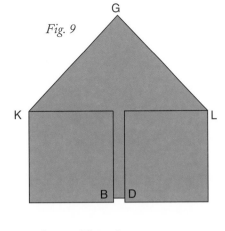

Fig. 9

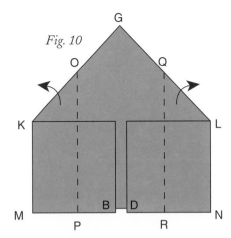

Fig. 10

Step 8. Repeat Step 7 with corner D (Figs. 8 and 9).

Step 9. Turn the paper over and repeat Steps 7 and 8.

Step 10. Fold back along OP and QR (Fig. 10) so that KM will be under flap OP and LN under flap QR (Fig. 11).

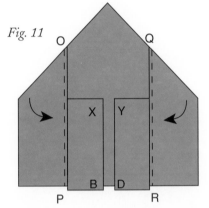

Fig. 11

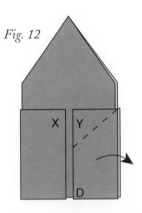

Fig. 12

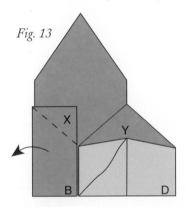

Fig. 13

Step 11. Turn the paper over and repeat Step 10 on the other side (Fig. 12).

Step 12. Open corner Y (Figs. 12 and 13).

Step 13. Open corner X (Figs. 13 and 14).

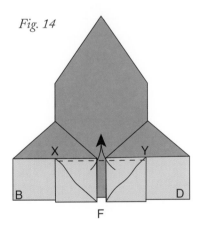

Fig. 14

Step 14. Fold along XY (Fig. 14), bringing point F up. Then turn the paper over and repeat Steps 12, 13 and 14. To complete the church, add the cross and draw the windows and doors.

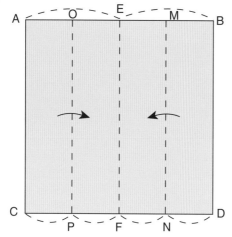

Fig. 1

Step 1. Fold a square piece of paper along lines OP and MN (Fig. 1) so that edges AC and BD meet at the center EF (Fig. 2).

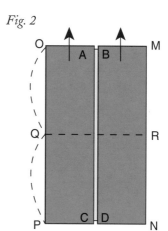

Fig. 2

Step 2. Fold OM back along QR (Fig. 2) so that OM will be under PN (Fig. 3).

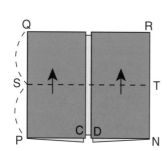

Fig. 3

Step 3. Fold along ST (Fig. 3) so that PN falls on QR (Fig. 4).

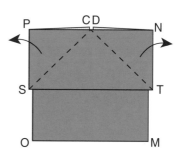

Fig. 4

Step 4. Make a crease along CS and DT (Fig. 4) and then pull out corners C and D (Fig. 5).

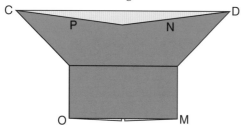

Fig. 5

Step 5. Turn the paper over and repeat Steps 3 and 4 (Fig. 6).

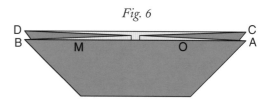

Fig. 6

Step 6. Spread out Fig. 6 so that it looks like Fig. 7.

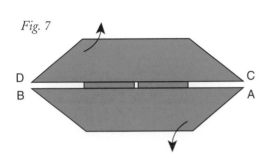

Fig. 7

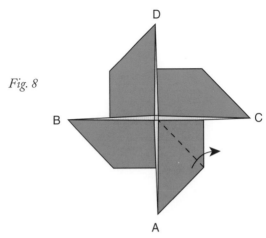

Fig. 8

Step 7. Fold D upwards and A downwards (Figs. 7 and 8) (see the "Windmill" on pages 26–27, Figs. 1–9).

Step 8. Open corner A (Fig. 8) and bring point A to the center (Fig. 9).

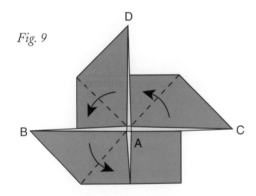

Fig. 9

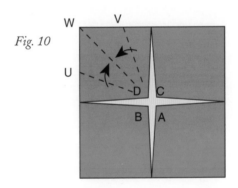

Fig. 10

Step 9. Repeat Step 8 at B, C, and D (Figs. 9 and 10).

Step 10. Fold along UD and VD (Fig. 10) so that XD and YD meet at the center WD (Fig. 11).

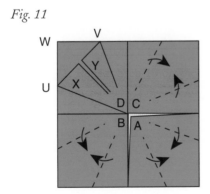

Fig. 11

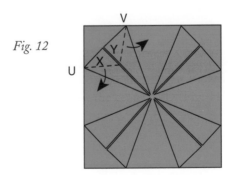

Fig. 12

Step 11. Repeat Step 10 on the other three squares (Figs. 11 and 12).

Step 12. Open corners X and Y (Fig. 12) and fold them flat (Fig. 13).

Fig. 13

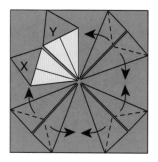

Fig. 14

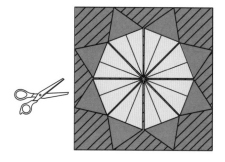

Step 13. Repeat Step 12 with the other six corners (Figs. 13 and 14).

Step 14. Cut off those portions shaded in (Fig. 14).

CLOCK

Fig. 1

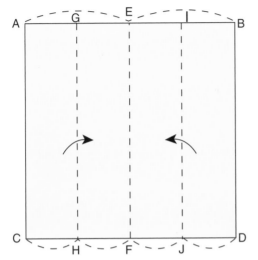

Step 1. Fold a square piece of paper along lines GH and IJ (Fig. 1) so that edges AC and BD meet at the center EF (Fig. 2).

Fig. 2

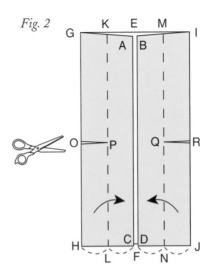

Step 2. Cut at OP and RQ, making GIRO an approximate square (Fig. 2).

Fig. 3

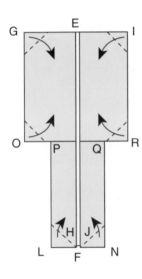

Step 3. Fold along PL and QN (Fig. 2) so that OH and RJ meet at EF (Fig. 3). Fold corners G, I, R and O forward (Figs. 3 and 5).

Fig. 4

Step 4. Fold corners L and N (Figs. 3 and 4) forward so that they meet on EF (Fig. 4).

Fig. 5

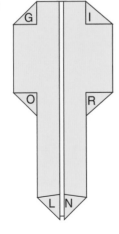

Step 5. Turn the paper over. Add a circle of white paper for the clock face and a rectangle of black paper below. Draw the face of the clock and the pendulum.

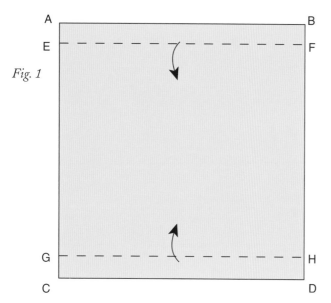

Fig. 1

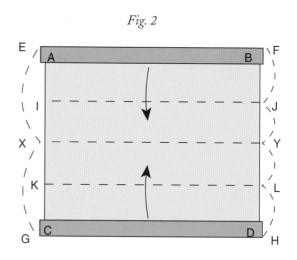

Fig. 2

Step 1. Fold in opposite ends of a square piece of paper about one-quarter of an inch from each edge along lines EF and GH (Figs. 1 and 2).

Step 2. Fold along IJ and KL (Fig. 2) so that EF and GH meet at the center XY (Fig. 3).

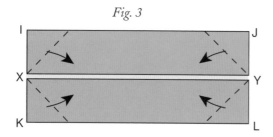

Fig. 3

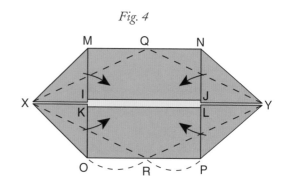

Fig. 4

Step 3. Fold corners I, J, K and L (Fig. 3) forward so that XI, YJ, XK and YL fall on XY (Fig. 4).

Step 4. Fold along XQ, QY, XR and RY (Fig. 4), bringing corners M, N, O and P forward (Fig. 5). Point Q and R are the corners of MN and OP respectively.

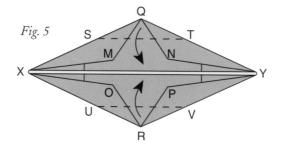

Fig. 5

Step 5. Fold along ST and UV (Fig. 5), bringing corners O and R forward (Fig. 6).

Fig. 6

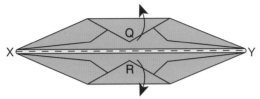

Fig. 7

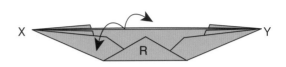

Step 6. Fold out in half along XY (Figs. 6 and 7).

Step 7. Take the two outer flaps (Fig. 7), one in each hand, and turn the entire object inside out (Fig. 8).

Fig. 8

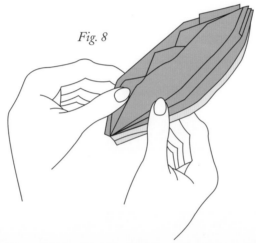

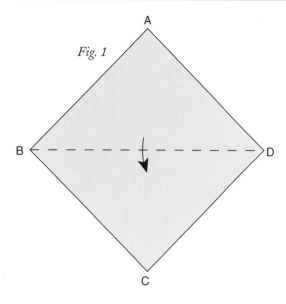

Fig. 1

Step 1. Fold a square piece of paper along line BD (Fig. 1) so that A falls on corner C (Fig. 2).

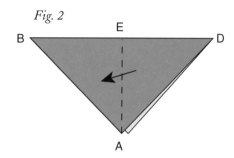

Fig. 2

Step 2. Fold along line EA (Fig. 2) so that corner D falls on B (Fig. 3).

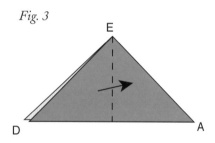

Fig. 3

Step 3. Open corner D (Fig. 3) and bring it over to the right until it is directly above A (Fig. 4).

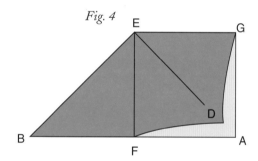

Fig. 4

Step 4. Crease along EF and EG (Fig. 5).

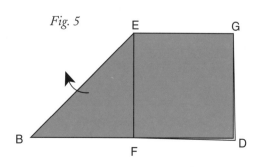

Fig. 5

Step 5. Turn the paper over and repeat Step 3 with B (Fig. 6).

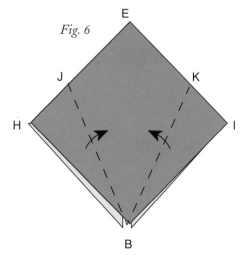

Fig. 6

Step 6. Fold along BJ and BK (Fig. 6) so that BH and BI meet at BE (Fig. 7) (see the "Crane" on page 30, Figs. 1–6).

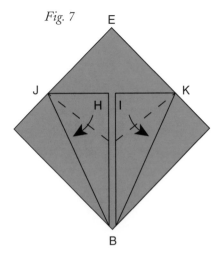

Fig. 7

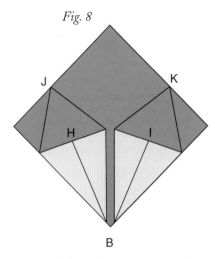

Fig. 8

Step 7. Open corner H and I (Fig. 7) so that JH falls on JB and KI on KB (Fig. 8).

Step 8. Turn the paper over and repeat Steps 5 and 6 (Fig. 9).

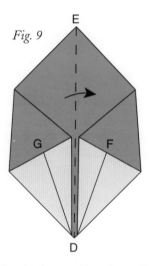

Fig. 9

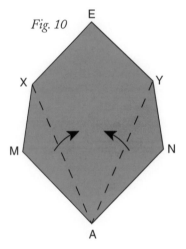

Fig. 10

Step 9. Fold only the top flap along ED (Fig. 9), and bring G on top of F. Then turn the paper over and bring I on top of H (Fig. 10).

Step 10. Fold along XA and YA (Fig. 10) so that MA and NA meet at EA (Fig. 11).

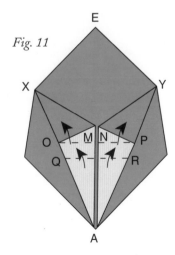

Fig. 11

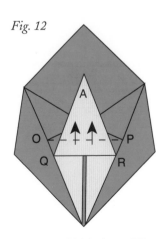

Fig. 12

Step 11. Fold along QR (Fig. 11), bringing A forward and up (Fig. 12).

Step 12. Fold along OP (Figs. 12 and 13).

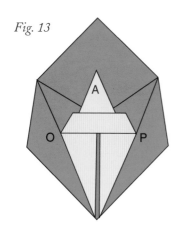

Fig. 13

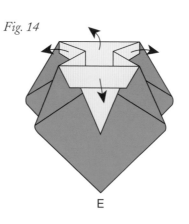

Fig. 14

Fig. 15

Step 13. Turn the paper over and repeat Steps 9, 10 and 11 on the other side with corner C, and then with B and D (Fig. 14).

Step 14. Carefully insert your fingers into the object and flatten E (Fig. 15).

TENT

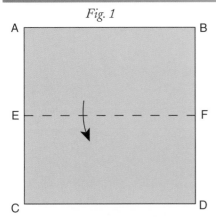
Fig. 1

Step 1. Fold a square piece of paper along line EF (Fig. 1) so that AB falls on CD (Fig. 2), and crease in the middle at GH.

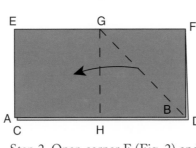
Fig. 2

Step 2. Open corner F (Fig. 2) and bring point F down between B and D so that GF falls on GH (Fig. 3). Crease GB and GD.

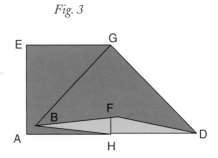
Fig. 3

Step 3. Turn the paper over and repeat Step 3 with E (Figs. 4 and 5).

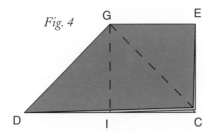
Fig. 4

Step 4. Fold along JK, JL and KM, making corners G, C and A meet on E, and then open (Fig. 5).

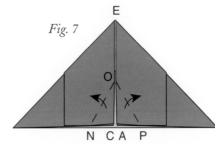
Fig. 5

Step 5. Lift up E so that it falls on G while corners C and A meet at the center (Fig. 6).

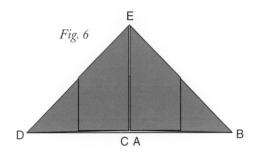
Fig. 6

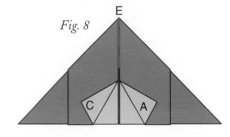
Fig. 7

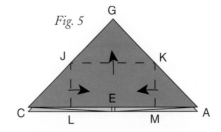
Fig. 8

Step 6. Fold along ON and OP and pull back the flaps (Figs. 7 and 8).

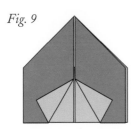
Fig. 9

Step 7. Turn the paper over and repeat Steps 5 and 6 on the other side.

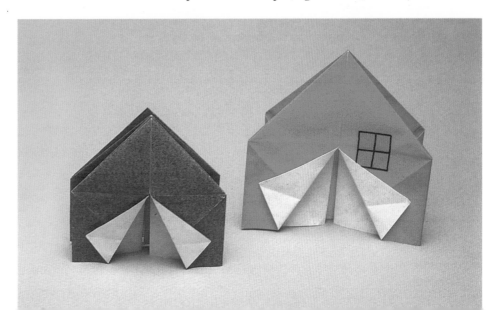

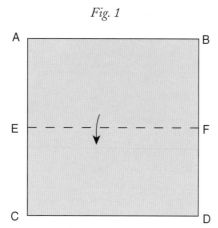

Fig. 1

Step 1. Fold a square piece of paper along line EF (Fig. 1) so that corner AB falls on CD (Fig. 2).

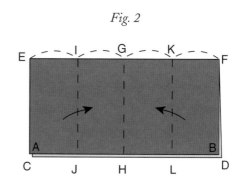

Fig. 2

Step 2. Fold along IJ and KL (Fig. 2) so that AEC and BFD meet at center GH (Fig. 3).

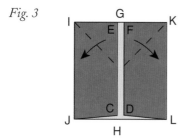

Fig. 3

Step 3. Open corner F (Fig. 3) by lifting D toward the right while holding B in place (Fig. 4).

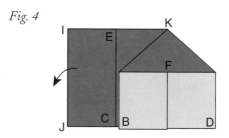

Fig. 4

Step 4. Repeat Step 3 with corner E (Figs. 4 and 5).

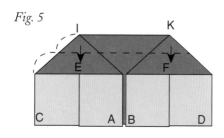

Fig. 5

Step 5. Fold along MN so that IK falls on EF (Fig. 6).

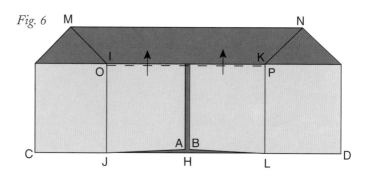

Fig. 6

Step 6. To make the keyboard, fold along OP (Fig. 6), bringing JHL forward (Fig. 7) and making OJ and PL at right angles to I and K.

Fig. 7

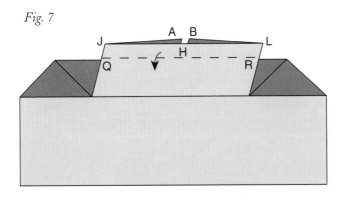

Fig. 8

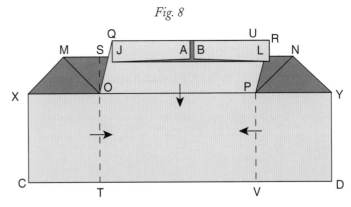

Step 7. Fold again at QR (Fig. 7), bringing JABL forward and down and forming right angles at Q and R (Fig. 8).

Step 8. Fold at ST, making XO touch OQ. Do the same for UV so that YP touches RP (Figs. 8 and 9), thus forming right angles at T and V.

Fig. 9

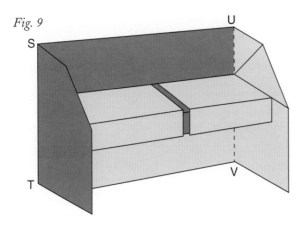

Step 9. Complete the piano by making black and white keys with paint or crayons (see the photograph below)

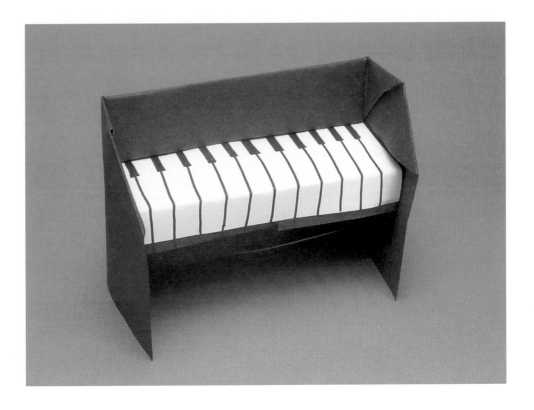

Nurse's Cap

Step 1. To make a "Nurse's Cap", repeat
Steps 1–4 in the "Piano", page 64.

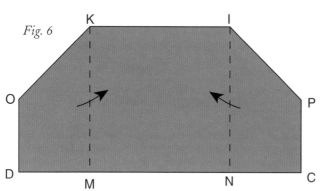

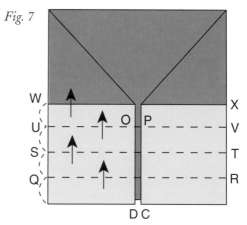

Step 2. Turn the paper over and fold along
KM and IN (Fig. 6) so that edges OD and
PC meet at the center (Fig. 7).

Step 3. Fold the top flap along QR,
then again at ST, at UV, and at WX
(Figs. 7 and 8).

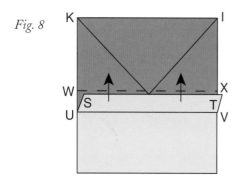

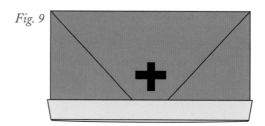

Step 4. Repeat Step 3
on the opposite flap.

Step 5. To complete the nurse's cap,
draw a cross in the center (Fig. 9).

Scout Cap or Billfold

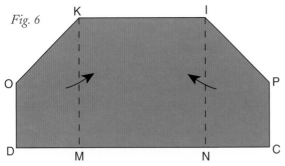

Fig. 6

Step 1. For the "Scout Cap" or "Billfold", repeat Steps 1 and 2 in the "Nurse's Cap" (Fig. 6).

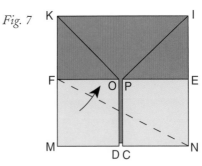

Fig. 7

Step 2. Fold the top flap along FN (Fig. 7).

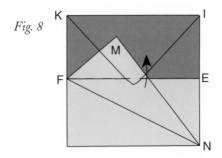

Fig. 8

Step 3. Fold again at FE (Fig. 8) so that point N falls on I (Fig. 9).

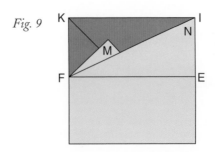

Fig. 9

Step 4. Do the same for the other flap.

Fig. 10

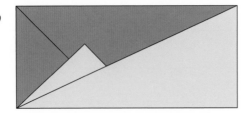

This is a billfold when closed. It can be worn as a Scout or a GI cap and, with the addition of a feather mark, it can be turned into a stewardess's cap.

BIRD

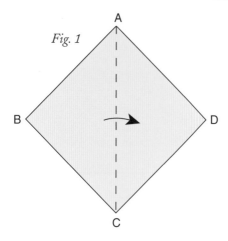

Step 1. Fold a square piece of paper along AC (Fig. 1) so that corner B falls on corner D (Fig. 2).

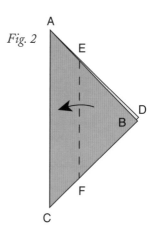

Step 2. Fold along EF (Fig. 2), bringing corners B and D to the left (Fig. 3). AE is a little less than one-half of the way down AD (Fig. 2).

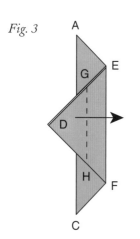

Step 3. Fold along GH (Fig. 3), bringing only corner D to the right while keeping B in place (Fig. 4).

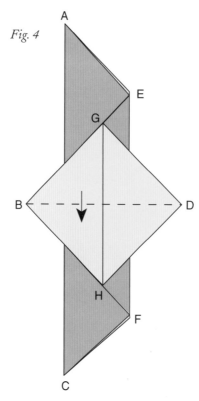

Step 4. Fold along BD (Fig. 4) so that edge AE falls on CF (Fig. 5).

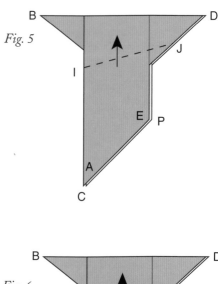

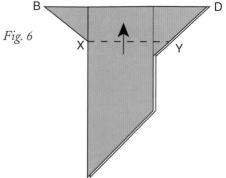

Step 5. Fold along IJ at a slant (Fig. 5) or horizontally along XY (Fig. 6) on the top flap of the body.

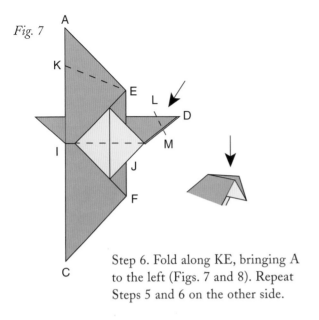

Fig. 7

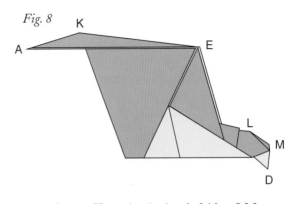

Fig. 8

Step 6. Fold along KE, bringing A to the left (Figs. 7 and 8). Repeat Steps 5 and 6 on the other side.

Step 7. To make the head, fold at LM (Fig. 7) and bring point D down between the flaps (Fig. 8).

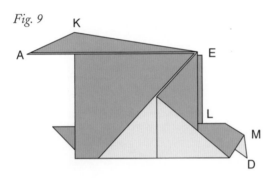

Fig. 9

If folding is done horizontally as in Fig. 6, the finished bird will look like the one in Fig. 9.

WHALE

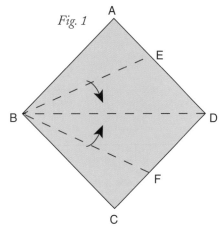

Fig. 1

Step 1. Fold a square piece of paper along BE and BF so that edges BA and BC meet at center line BD (Figs. 1 and 2).

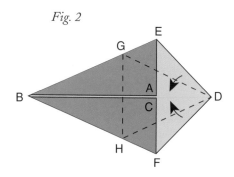

Fig. 2

Step 2. Fold along GD and HD (Fig. 2) so that ED and FD meet at center line BD (Fig. 3).

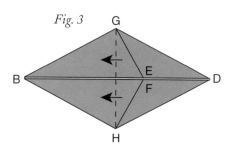

Fig. 3

Step 3. Pull out corners A and C so that they meet at center line BD (Fig. 4).

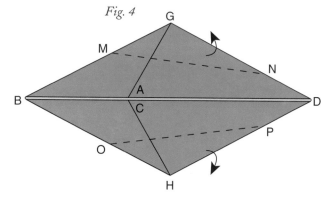

Fig. 4

Step 4. Fold back along MN and OP so that G and H meet at the center line on the other side (Fig. 5).

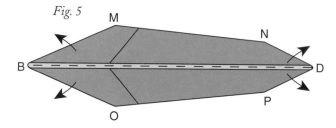

Fig. 5

Step 5. Fold in half along BD to make the body (Fig. 6).

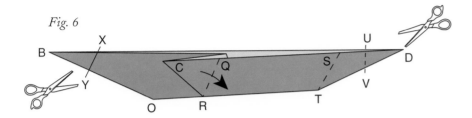

Fig. 6

Step 6. To make the fins, fold at QR, bringing corner O downward and away from the body (Fig. 6). Do the same for the other side.

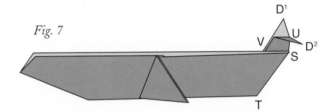

Fig. 7

Step 7. To make the tail, fold back along ST (Fig. 6). Make a slit at UD and open D1 and D2 at VU (Fig. 7).

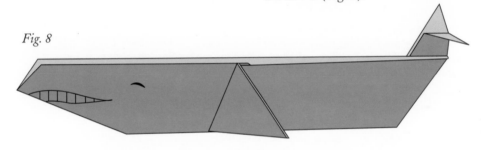

Fig. 8

Step 8. Cut off point B at XY (Fig. 6) and draw the mouth and eyes (Fig. 8).

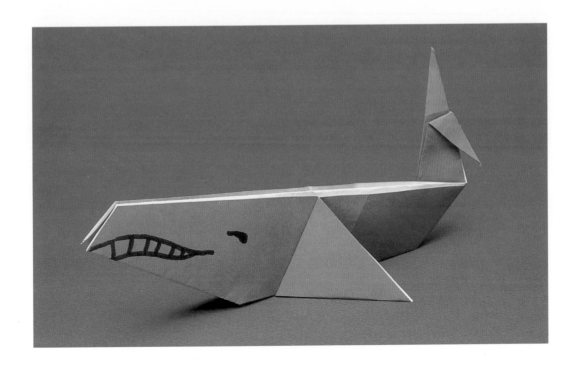

SWALLOW

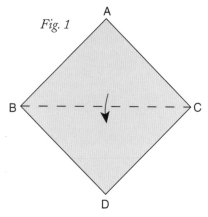

Fig. 1

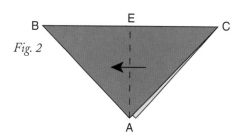

Fig. 2

Fig. 3

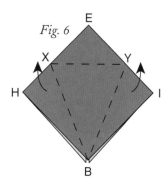

Step 2. Fold along EA (Fig. 2) so that point C falls on B (Fig. 3).

Step 1. Fold a square piece of paper along line BC (Fig. 1) so that corner A falls on corner D (Fig. 2).

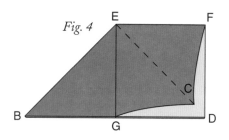

Fig. 4

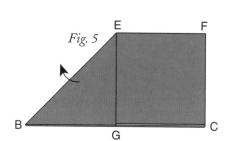

Fig. 5

Fig. 6

Step 3. Open C and bring it over to the right directly above D (Fig. 4). Place C on D and crease EF and EG (Fig. 5).

Step 4. Turn the paper over and repeat Step 3 with B (Figs. 5 and 6).

Step 5. Crease at XB and YB (Fig. 6) so that HB and IB meet at center EB, and open.

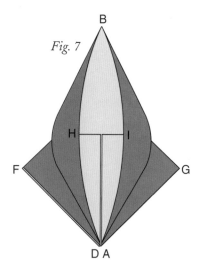

Fig. 7

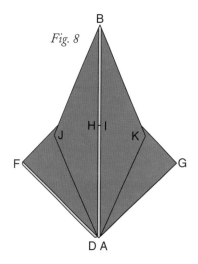

Fig. 8

Fig. 9

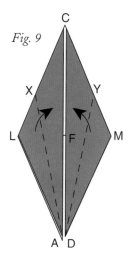

Fig. 10

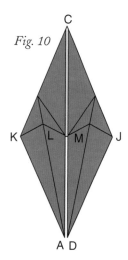

Step 6. Lift up B and fold at XY (Fig. 6) so that H and I meet at the middle on BD and BA respectively (Figs. 7 and 8).

Step 7. Turn the paper over and repeat Steps 5 and 6 on the other side (Fig. 9).

Step 8. Fold along XA and YD (Fig. 9) so that L and M meet at the center on top of G and F (Fig. 10).

Step 9. Turn the paper over and repeat Step 8 on the other side for K and J (Fig. 11).

Fig. 11

Step 10. Take the top flap and fold to the left, making K fall on J (Fig. 11).

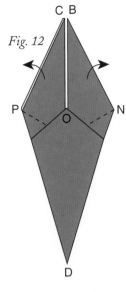

Fig. 12

Step 11. Repeat the same on the other side, making M fall on L (Fig. 12).

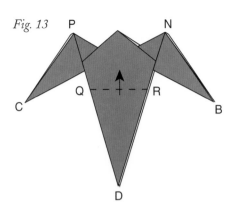

Fig. 13

Step 12. To make the wings, bring B down to the right in between the two flaps and fold at ON (Figs. 12 and 13). Do the same for C, folding at OP (Fig. 13).

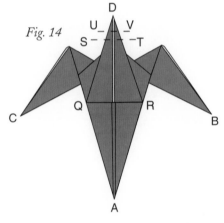

Fig. 14

Step 13. Lift D to the front and up, folding at QR (Figs. 13 and 14).

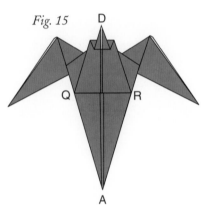

Fig. 15

Step 14. To make the head, fold along ST, bringing D forward and down. Fold again at UV, making D point D upward (Fig. 15).

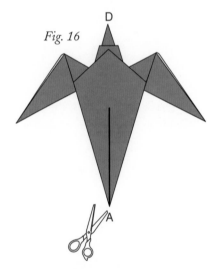

Fig. 16

Step 15. Turn the paper over. Cut one-third of the way up along AD from A (Fig. 16).

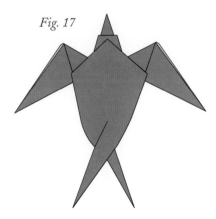

Fig. 17

Step 16. Make both parts of the tail cross each other (Fig. 17).

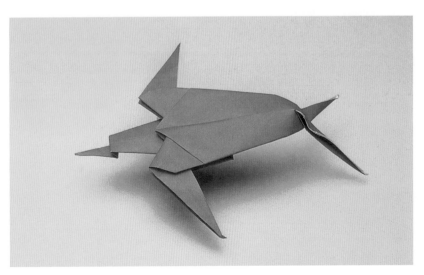

FROG

Fig. 1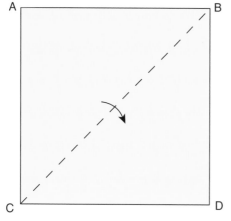

Step 1. Fold a square piece of paper along line BC (Fig. 1) so that corner A falls on corner D (Fig. 2).

Fig. 2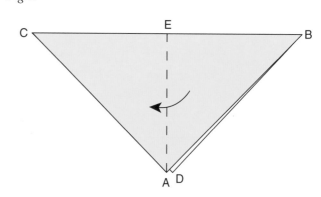

Step 2. Fold along EA (Fig. 2) so that point B falls on C (Fig. 3).

Fig. 3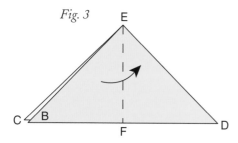

Step 3. Open B (Fig. 3) and bring it over to the right, directly above D (Fig. 4). Place B on D and crease EF and EG.

Fig. 4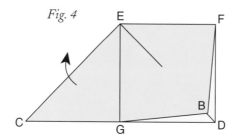

Fig. 5

Step 4. Turn the paper over and repeat Step 3 with C (Figs. 4 and 5).

Fig. 6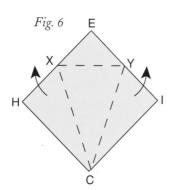

Step 5. Crease at XC and YC (Fig. 6) so that edges HC and IC meet along center line EC, and open.

Fig. 7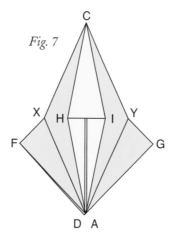

Step 6. Lift up C and fold at XY (Fig. 6) so that H and I meet at the middle on CD and CA respectively (Figs. 7 and 8).

Fig. 8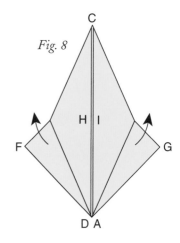

Step 7. Turn the paper over and repeat Steps 5 and 6 (Fig. 9).

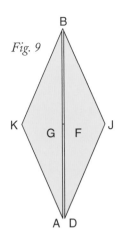

Fig. 9

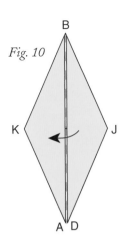

Fig. 10

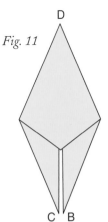

Fig. 11

Step 8. Fold top flap to the left (Fig. 10) so that J falls on top of K.

Step 9. Turn over and repeat Step 8 on the other side (Fig. 10) and turn figure upside down (Fig. 11).

Step 10. To make the hind legs, lift B back between the flaps and to the right, and C to the left (Figs. 12 and 13).

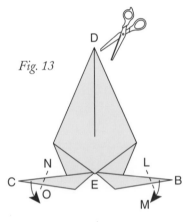

Fig. 13

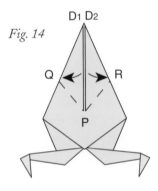

Fig. 14

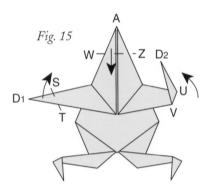

Fig. 15

Step 11. Fold along LM and NO so that B and C are bent forward again on both sides (Figs. 13 and 14).

Step 12. Cut the top flap only from D toward E about two-thirds of the way down the body flap (Fig. 13).

Step 13. Fold along PQ and PR (Fig. 14) so that corners D1 and D2 stretch out on both sides of the body flap (Fig. 15).

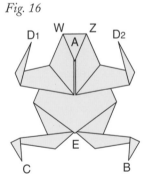

Fig. 16

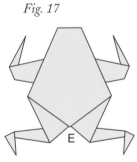

Fig. 17

Step 14. Fold ST and UV (Fig. 15), making the two points D1 and D2 face upward towards A (Fig. 16).

Step 15. Fold along WZ so that corner A comes down to the front (Fig. 16). Turn over (Fig. 17).

Make the frog move by tapping at E (Fig. 17) with your forefinger. You can also make several frogs and have a frog race with your friends and see whose frog wins the race.

PRINCE AND PRINCESS

Prince

Fig. 1

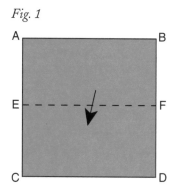

Step 1. To make the "Prince", fold a square sheet of paper along line EF (Fig. 1) so that AB falls on CD (Fig. 2).

Fig. 2

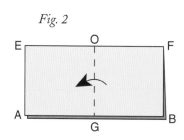

Step 2. Fold along OG (Fig. 2) so that FB falls on EA, then open (Fig. 3).

Fig. 3

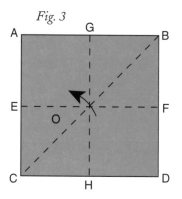

Step 3. Fold along CB (Fig. 3) so that D falls on A (Fig. 4).

Fig. 4

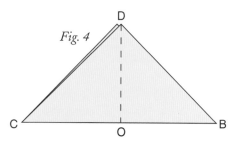

Step 4. Fold along DO so that B falls on C (Fig. 4), then open (Fig. 5).

Fig. 5

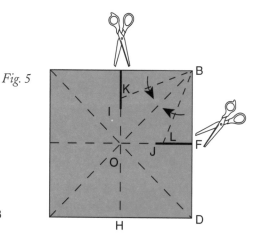

Step 5. Cut along GI and FJ, each cut being a little less than two-thirds of the way towards the center O (Fig. 5).

Fig. 6

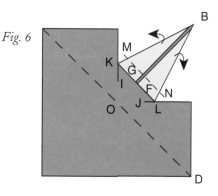

Step 6. Fold along KB and LB so that GB meets BF at center BO (Figs. 5 and 6).

Fig. 7

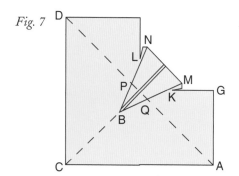

Step 7. Fold back along MN (Fig. 6) and turn the paper over so that B falls on OC (Fig. 7). MN is less than two-thirds of the way down BO.

Fig. 8

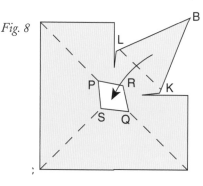

Step 8. Mark PQ along DA (Fig. 7) and cut out diamond shape PRQS, R and S being on BC (Fig. 8).

Fig. 9

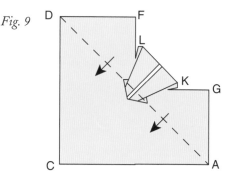

Step 9. Bring point B forward through opening PRQS (Fig. 9).

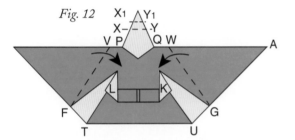

Fig. 10

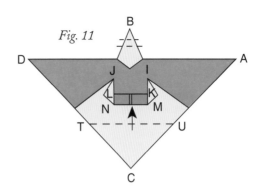

Fig. 11

Step 10. Fold along DA (Fig. 9), bringing F and G forward, and point B will come up by itself (Fig. 10).

Step 11. Fold along JN and IM (Fig. 10), opening L and K (Fig. 11). Fold along TU (Fig. 11), putting C under the front body flap (Fig. 12).

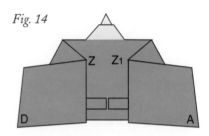

Fig. 12

Fig. 13

Fig. 14

Step 12. Fold along VF and WG (Fig. 12), bringing points D and A forward, V and W being nearly half an inch from P and Q respectively (Fig. 13).

Step 13. Make the head piece by folding along XY, bringing point B back along OC (Fig. 12), then again at X₁ Y₁, bringing B up (Fig. 13).

Step 14. Fold along ZH (Fig. 13), opening corner D so that DZ falls on HZ. Do the same for A, folding along Z₁F (Fig. 14).

Princess

To make the "Princess", repeat Steps 1–6 of the "Prince" (Figs. 1–6) and follow the diagrams closely from Fig. 7 on. The main difference is the cutting of the notches to make the head piece. With another piece of paper, make a pleated paper fan for the princess (see the "Fan" on page 8).

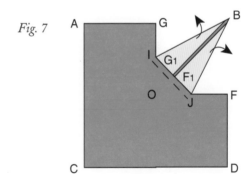

Fig. 7

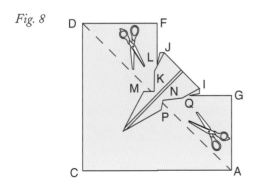

Fig. 8

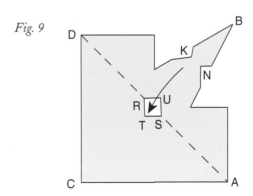

Fig. 9

Fig. 10

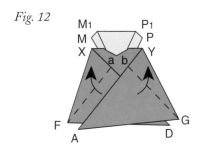

Fig. 11

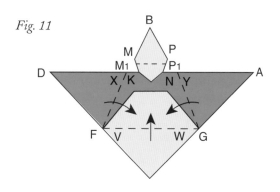

Fig. 12

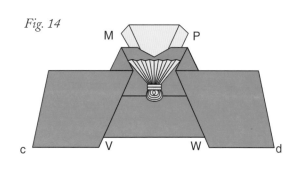

Fig. 13

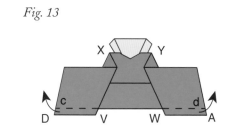

Fan

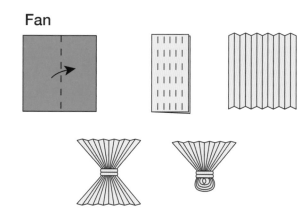

Fig. 14

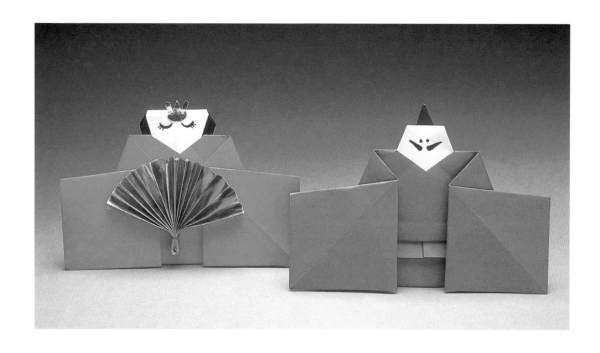

PIG

Fig. 1

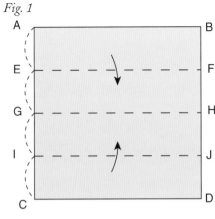

Fig. 2

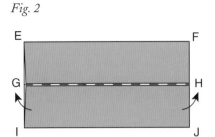

Step 1. Fold a square piece of paper along EG and IJ so that edges AB and CD meet at center GH (Figs. 1 and 2).

Step 2. Fold in half along GH (Fig. 2) so that IJ falls on the back side of EF (Fig. 3).

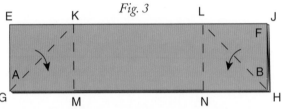

Fig. 3

Fig. 4

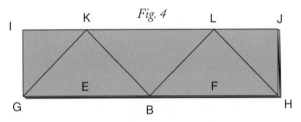

Step 3. Take the front flap and open corners E and F (Fig. 3) by bringing A to the right and B to the left so that they meet each other along HG. EK falls on MK and FL on NL respectively (Fig. 4).

Step 4. Turn over and repeat Step 3 with I and J (Fig. 5).

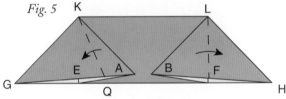

Fig. 5

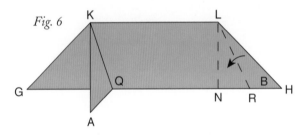

Fig. 6

Step 5. Fold along KQ (Fig. 5) so that KA falls on KE (Fig. 6).

Step 6. Move B to the right (Fig. 5) so that edge LB falls on LH (Fig. 6). Fold along LR (Fig. 6) so that LH falls on LN.

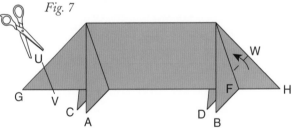

Fig. 7

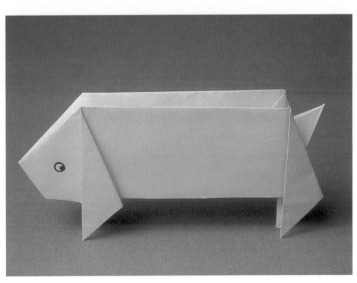

Step 7. Turn over and repeat Steps 5, 6 and 7 (Fig. 7). Cut off point G at UV and draw dots for the eyes (Figs. 7 and 8).

Fig. 8

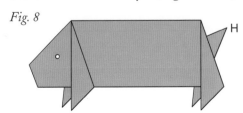

Step 8. To make the tail, fold along WF (Fig. 7) and push H in between the body flaps (Fig. 8).

Fig. 1

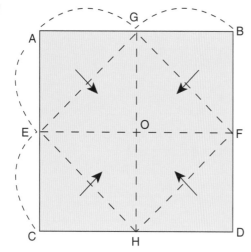

Step 1. Fold a square piece of paper along EG, GF and HE so that corners A, B, C and D will all meet at center point O (Figs. 1 and 2).

Fig. 2

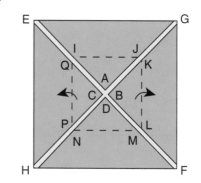

Step 2. Fold along IJ, KL, MN and PQ (Fig. 2) so that corners A and D are inside the flap (Fig. 3) touching edges EG and HF respectively, while corners C and B touch edges EH and GF from the outside (Fig. 3).

Fig. 3

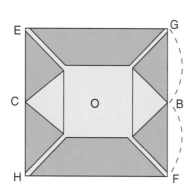

Fig. 4

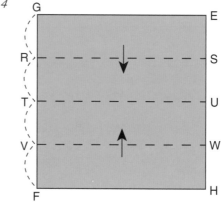

Step 3. Turn over. Fold along RS and VW (Fig. 4) so that edges GE and FH meet at center TU (Fig. 5).

Fig. 5

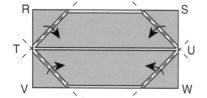

Step 4. Fold corners R, S, V and W forward (Fig. 5) so that RT, SU, TV and UW fall on TU (Fig. 6).

Fig. 6

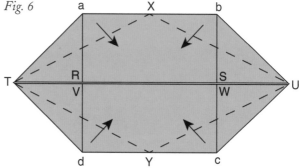

Step 5. Fold along TX, XU, UY and TY (Fig. 6), bringing corners a, b, c and d forward (Fig. 7). Points X and Y are centers of ab and cd respectively.

Fig. 7

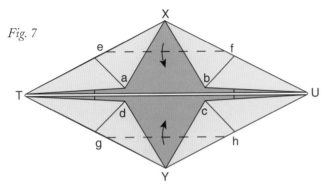

Step 6. Fold along ef and gh (Fig. 7), bringing corners X and Y forward (Fig. 8).

Fig. 8

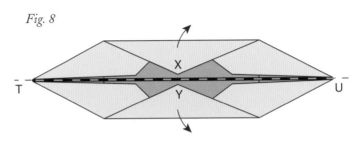

Step 7. Fold out in half along TU (Figs. 8 and 9).

Fig. 9

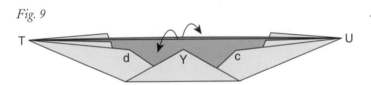

Step 8. Take the two outer flaps (Fig. 9), one in each hand, and turn the entire object inside out (Fig. 10).

Fig. 10

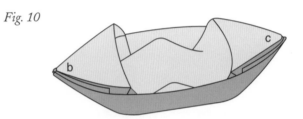

81

Fig. 1

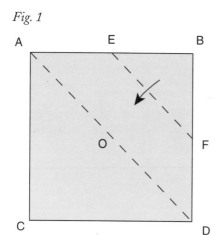

Step 1. Fold a square piece of paper along EF (Fig. 1) so that corner B meets center O (Fig. 2).

Fig. 2

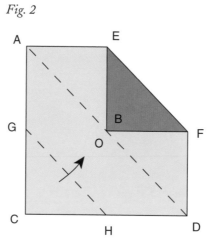

Step 2. Fold along GH (Fig. 2) so that corner C meets B at center O (Fig. 3).

Fig. 3

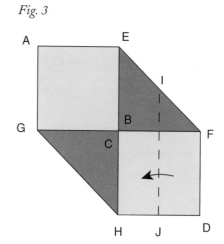

Step 3. Fold along IJ (Fig. 3) so that edge FD meets CH (Fig. 4).

Fig. 4

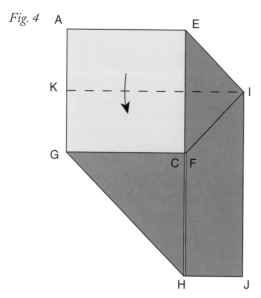

Step 4. Fold along KI (Fig. 4) so that edge AE meets GC (Fig. 5).

Fig. 5

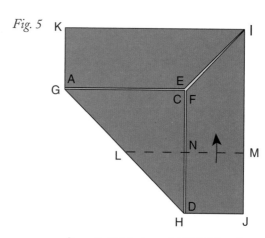

Step 5. Fold along LNM (Fig. 5) so that edge D falls on F (Fig. 6).

Fig. 6

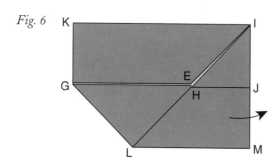

Fig. 7

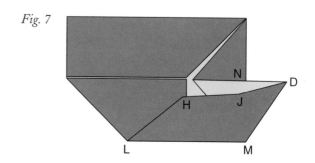

Step 6. Open corner J, bringing corner D to the right, thus making MJ fall on MN (Fig. 7).

Fig. 8

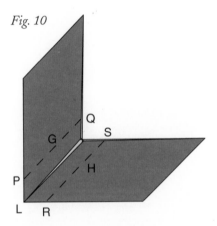

Step 7. Repeat Steps 5 and 6 with A (Figs. 8 and 9).

Fig. 9

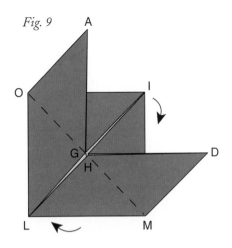

Step 8. Fold back I along OM so that I falls underneath L (Fig. 9).

Fig. 10

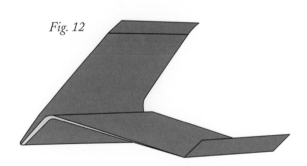

Step 9. Fold along PQ and RS so that the two touch each other (Fig. 10).

Fig. 11

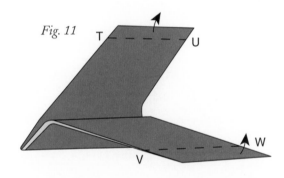

Step 10. Fold along TU and VW (Fig. 11) so that the two edges turn up (Figs. 11 and 12).

Fig. 12

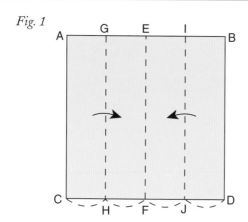

Fig. 1

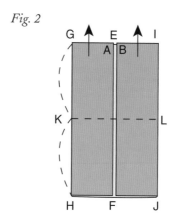

Fig. 2

Step 1. Fold a square piece of paper along GH and IJ (Fig. 1) so that edges AC and BD meet at center EF (Fig. 2).

Step 2. Fold GI back along KL (Fig. 2) so that GI will be under HJ (Fig. 3).

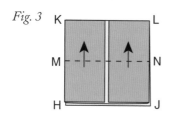

Fig. 3

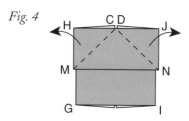

Fig. 4

Step 3. Fold the top flap along MN (Fig. 3) so that HJ falls on KL (Fig. 4).

Step 4. Make a crease along CM and DN (Fig. 4) and then pull out corners C and D (Fig. 5).

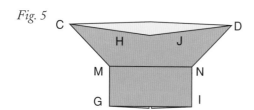

Fig. 5

Fig. 6

Step 5. Turn the paper over and repeat Steps 3 and 4.

Step 6. Spread out Fig. 6 so that it looks like Fig. 7.

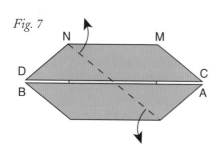

Fig. 7

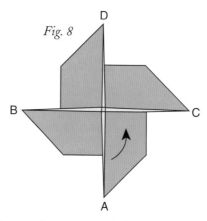

Fig. 8

Step 7. Fold D upward and A downward (Figs. 7 and 8).

Step 8. Open corner A (Fig. 8) and bring point A to the center (Fig. 9) (see the "Windmill" on pages 26–27, Figs. 1–9).

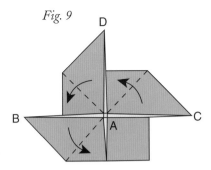

Fig. 9

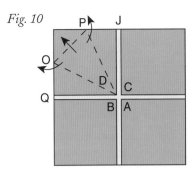

Fig. 10

Step 9. Repeat Step 8 at B, C and D (Figs. 9 and 10).

Step 10. Crease at OD and PD (Fig. 10) so that QD and JD meet at the center. Then crease at OP. Lift up D, folding along OP so that Q and J meet at the middle (Fig. 11) on DZ.

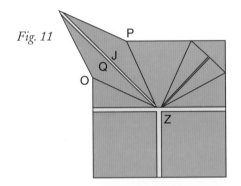

Fig. 11

Step 11. Repeat Step 10 for other corners A, B and C (Figs. 11 and 12).

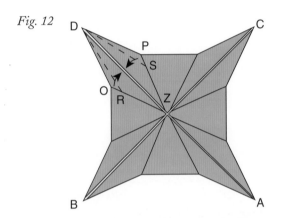

Fig. 12

Step 12. Fold along DR and DS (Fig. 12) so that DO meets DP at the center on DZ. Repeat Step 12 on A, B, and C (Fig. 13).

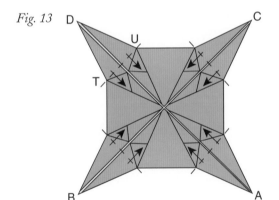

Fig. 13

Step 13. To make the legs stand, fold D along TU (Fig. 13).

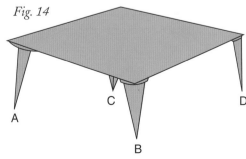

Fig. 14

Step 14. Repeat Step 13 on C, A and B (Fig. 14).

SPACE SHIP

Fig. 1

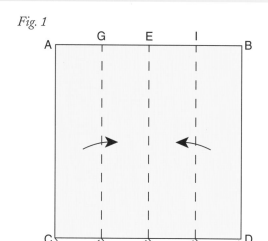

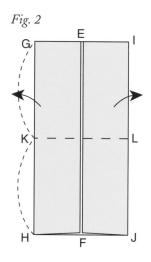

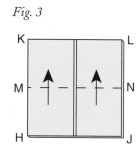

Step 1. Fold a square piece of paper along GH and IJ (Fig. 1) so that AC and BD meet at center EF (Fig. 2).

Step 2. Fold GI back along KL (Fig. 2) so that GI will be under HJ (Fig. 3).

Step 3. Fold along MN (Fig. 3) so that HJ falls on KL (Fig. 4).

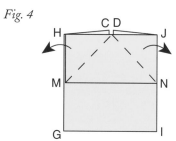

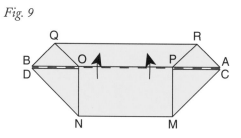

Step 4. Crease at CM and DN (Fig. 4) and then pull out corners C and D, thus opening H and J (Fig. 5). Turn over and repeat Steps 3 and 4.

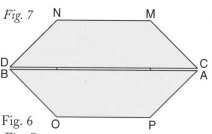

Step 5. Spread out Fig. 6 so that it looks like Fig. 7.

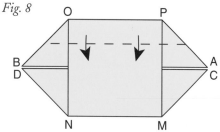

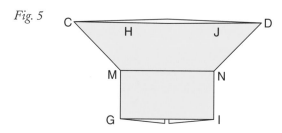

Step 6. Turn paper over (Fig. 8). Fold along QR so that OP falls on BA (Fig. 9).

Step 7. Fold along center (Fig. 9) so that DC falls on BA (Fig. 10).

Fig. 10

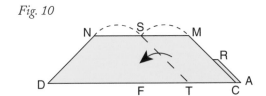

Step 8. Fold along ST (Fig. 10)
so that SM falls on SF (Fig. 11).

Fig. 11

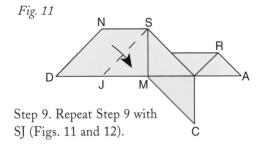

Step 9. Repeat Step 9 with
SJ (Figs. 11 and 12).

Fig. 12

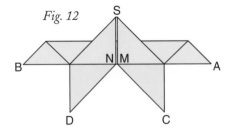

Fig. 13

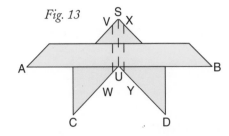

Step 10. Turn over (Fig. 13). Fold along
VW and XY so that they meet (Fig. 14).

Fig. 14

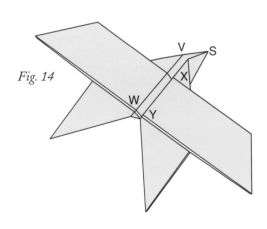

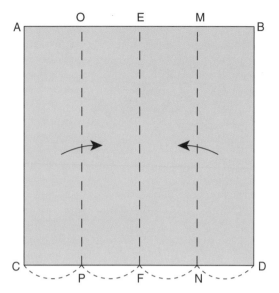

Fig. 1

Step 1. Fold a square piece of paper along lines OP and MN (Fig. 1) so that edges AC and BD meet at center EF (Fig. 2).

Fig. 2

Step 2. Fold OM back along QR (Fig. 2) so that OM will be under PN (Fig. 3).

Fig. 3

Step 3. Fold along ST (Fig. 3) so that PN falls on QR (Fig. 4).

Fig. 4

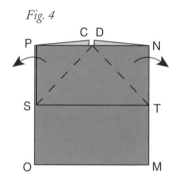

Step 4. Make a crease along CS and DT (Fig. 4) and then pull out corners C and D.

Fig. 5

Step 5. Turn the paper over and repeat Steps 3 and 4 (Fig. 6).

Fig. 6

Step 6. Spread out Fig. 6 so that it looks like Fig. 7.

Fig. 7

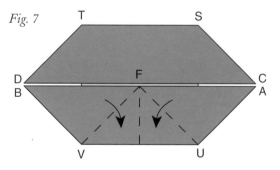

Step 7. Fold along FV and FU, bringing B and A downward to meet at the center (Figs. 7 and 8).

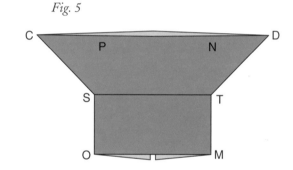

Fig. 8

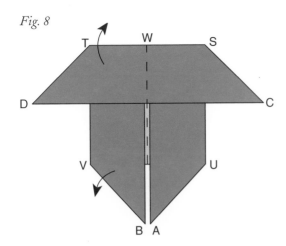

Step 8. Fold in half along WA so that S and T, C and D, U and V meet respectively (Fig. 9).

Fig. 9

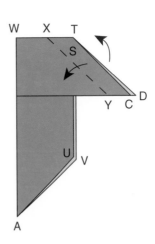

Step 9. Fold along XY, bringing S and C in front (Figs. 9 and 10).

Fig. 10

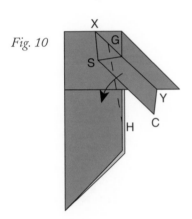

Step 10. Fold again at GH, bringing YC forward (Fig. 11).

Fig. 11

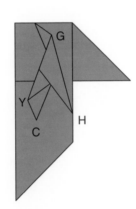

Step 11. Repeat Steps 9 and 10 on other side of body flap (Fig. 12).

Fig. 12

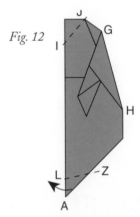

Step 12. To make the head, fold along IJ and KJ (Fig. 13) pushing IJ back in between the body flaps (Fig. 14).

Fig. 13

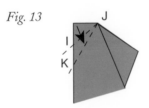

Step 13. To make the feet, fold along LZ (Fig. 12), putting A in between body flaps.

Fig. 14

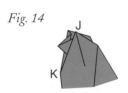

Step 14. Do the same on the other side (Fig. 15).

Fig. 15

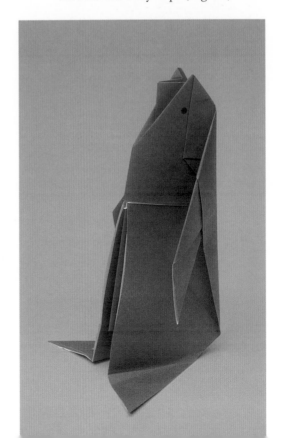

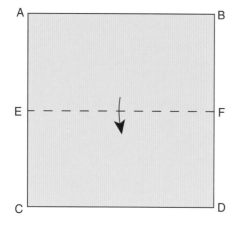

Step 1. Fold a square piece of paper along EF (Fig. 1) so that AB falls on CD (Fig. 2).

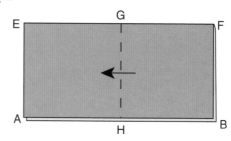

Step 2. Fold along GH so that FB falls on EA (Fig. 2). Fold in half again, then open (Fig. 3).

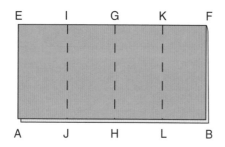

Step 3. Fold forward along YM and NZ (Fig. 4) so that EM and NF fall on MO and NP respectively. Then open. M and N are halfway between IG and GK (Figs. 4 and 5).

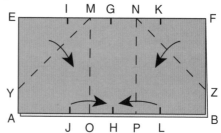

Step 4. Fold along IJ and KL so that the two edges fall on center GH (Figs. 4 and 5).

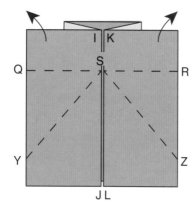

Step 5. Fold back along QSR and open (Fig. 5).

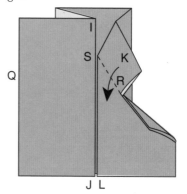

Step 6. Open corner K so that SR falls on top of SL (Figs. 5, 6 and 7).

Fig. 7

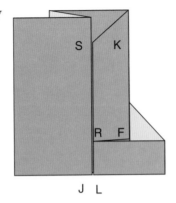

Step 7. Repeat Step 6 with corner I (Fig. 8).

Fig. 8

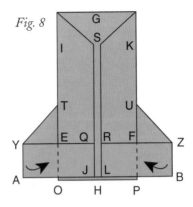

Step 8. By lifting the top flaps at EQRF, crease along IO and KP (Fig. 8) so that AO and PB form right angles to OI and LP respectively (Figs. 9 and 10).

Fig. 9

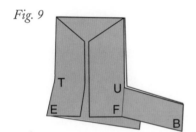

Fig. 10

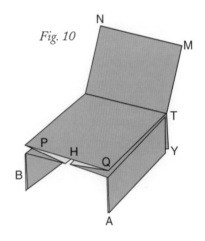

Fig. 1

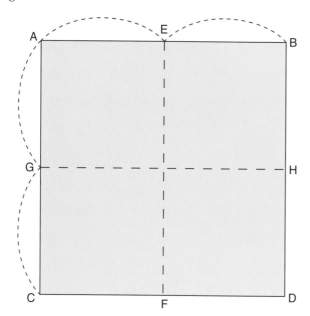

Fig. 2

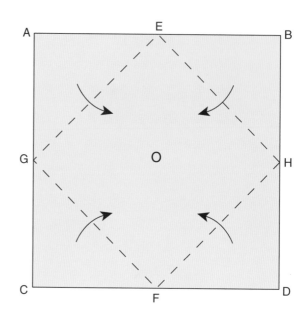

Step 1. Fold a square piece of paper along EH, HF, GF and EG (Figs. 1 and 2) so that corners A, B, C and D meet at center O (Fig. 3). E, F, G and H are center points of each edge.

Step 2. Crease along IJ, KL, MN and OP (Fig. 3), each crease being just a little less than halfway in towards the center.

Fig. 3

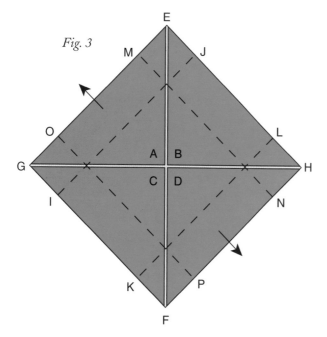

Step 3. Open out corners A and D as in Fig. 4.

Fig. 4

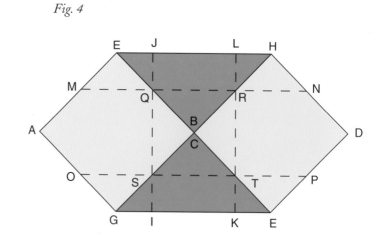

Step 4. Fold along MN and OP (Fig. 4) and push in corners H and F so that LR meets RN and TK meets TP (Fig. 5).

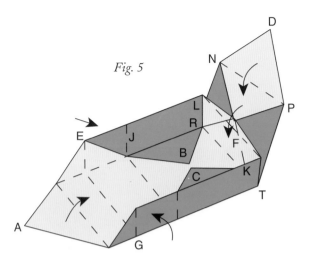

Fig. 5

Step 5. Fold along LK so that NP falls on RT and corner D meets B and C at the center (Fig. 5).

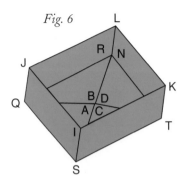

Fig. 6

Step 6. Repeat Steps 4 and 5 with corners E, G and A (Fig. 6).

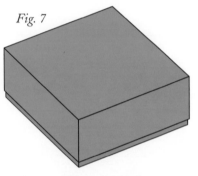

Fig. 7

Step 7. Decorate the box whichever way you like.

Note: By using square papers of different sizes you can get one box to fit over the other like a lid. You can also make a nest of boxes of all sizes, one inside the other.

USING ORIGAMI OBJECTS

Party

On pages 94–96 you will find different ways of using origami objects which you have learned to fold. Here are some party suggestions. These figures are all from the book. See if you can think of other ways to use these paper creations.

1. Lantern, p. 22
2. Flower, p. 54
3. Windmill, p. 26
4. Clown, p. 47
5. Flowers, p. 14
6. Treasure Box, p. 92
7. Swan, p. 28
8. Crane, p. 30
9. Wolf, p. 34
10. Caps, p. 66
11. Cat, p. 46
12. Helmet, p. 18
13. Dog, p. 33
14. Rabbit, p. 44

Mobile

Make an origami mobile by stringing various objects of different sizes and colors to thin pieces of wire. The mobile shown here features birds, but any of the objects you have learned to fold can be used.

1. Swan, p. 28
2. Penguin, p. 88
3. Robin, p. 50
4. Peahen, p. 37
5. Peacock, p. 36
6. Swallow, p. 72
7. Crane, p. 30

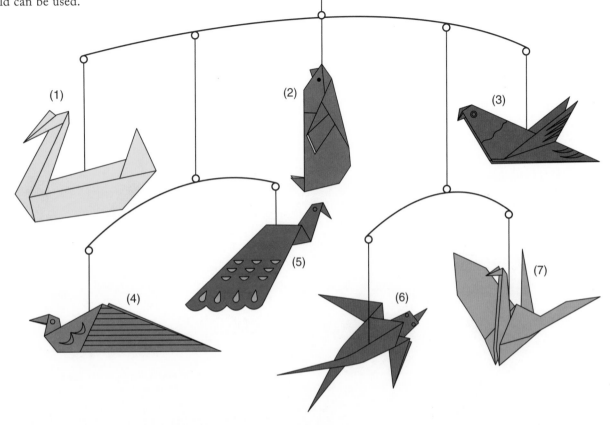

Boat Race

Make boats of various sizes and colors. Tie one end of a piece of string to each boat and the other end to the middle of a pencil. At the starting signal, each player winds the string on his pencil, thus pulling his boat towards him. The first boat reaching the finishing line wins the race.

1. Motorboat, p. 80
2. Rowboat, p. 58

Hunting Game

Arrange various origami objects on a table. Put point marks on each object as shown here. Stand at a distance from the table and, with a rubber band as a slingshot, shoot these objects and let them fall. The one who gets the most points is the best hunter. Besides this hunting game, you can also make a miniature zoo with the different animals shown in the book.

1. Penguin, p. 86
2. Whale, p. 70
3. Giraffe, p. 38
4. Peahen, p. 37
5. Pig, p. 79
6. Christmas Tree, p. 12
7. Elephant, p. 40
8. Rabbit, p. 44
9. Tent, p. 63
10. Wolf, p. 34

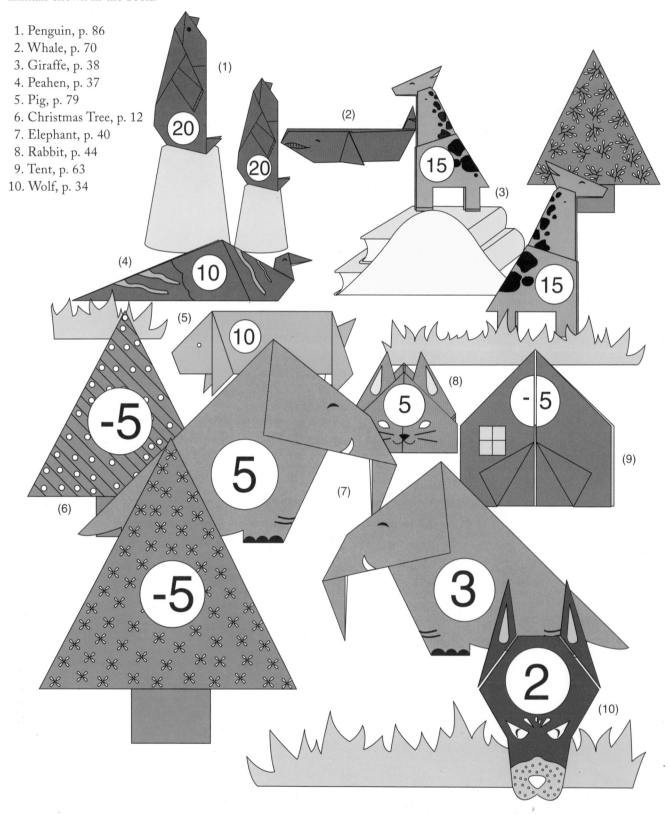